The Inter-American Development Bank

Sidney Dell

The Inter-American Development Bank

A Study in Development Financing

PRAEGER SPECIAL STUDIES IN INTERNATIONAL ECONOMICS AND DEVELOPMENT

Praeger Publishers New York Washington London

PRAEGER PUBLISHERS
111 Fourth Avenue, New York, N.Y. 10003, U.S.A.
5, Cromwell Place, London S.W.7, England

Published in the United States of America in 1972
by Praeger Publishers, Inc.

© 1972 by Sidney Dell

Library of Congress Catalog Card Number: 70-185778

Printed in the United States of America

For Ethel

This book is the result of a suggestion from Felipe Herrera at the time when he was President of the Inter-American Development Bank. The book reviews the policies of the IDB in relation to the purposes for which it was founded and its role in Latin American development. It does not seek to provide an evaluation of IDB projects as carried out; any such evaluation would require extensive field surveys, which the author was not in a position to undertake.

The book could not have been written without the help of members of the IDB staff, who provided the author with statistical and other material and who responded with care and patience to a large number of questions addressed to them at various times; particularly valuable advice and assistance were received from Osvaldo Básquez, Alberto Calvo, José Epstein, Cristián Santa Cruz, and Arnold Weiss. The World Bank also provided helpful comments and suggestions. The author owes much to a volume of essays on the work of the IDB entitled Una Década de Lucha por América Latina, published by the Fondo de Cultura Económica. He also gratefully acknowledges valuable comments received from Robert Asher, Diego Cordovez, and John White. The author alone is responsible for any errors that remain.

The views expressed in the book are those of the author and do not necessarily represent those of the IDB, or of the U.N. Secretariat to which he belongs.

CONTENTS

LIST OF TABLES

LIST OF ABBREVIATIONS

ADB	Asian Development Bank
ADELA	ADELA Investment Company
AID	Agency for International Development (United States)
CABEI	Central American Bank for Economic Integration
CACM	Central American Common Market
CARIBANK	Caribbean Development Bank
CELADE	Latin American Center for Demography
CIAP	Inter-American Committee for the Alliance for Progress
CIDA	Canadian International Development Agency
DAC	Development Assistance Committee (of the OECD)
ECLA	Economic Commission for Latin America
EDC	Export Development Corporation (Canada)
EDF	European Development Fund
EEC	European Economic Community
EFTA	European Free Trade Association
EXIMBANK	Export-Import Bank (United States)
FSO	Fund for Special Operations (of the IDB)
IBRD	International Bank for Reconstruction and Development (World Bank)
IDA	International Development Association
IDB	Inter-American Development Bank
IFC	International Finance Corporation
ILPES	Latin American Institute for Economic and Social Planning
IMF	International Monetary Fund
INTAL	Institute for Latin American Integration
LAFTA	Latin American Free Trade Association
OAS	Organization of American States
OECD	Organization for Economic Cooperation and Development

SIECA	Permanent Secretariat for Central American Economic Integration (of the CACM)
SPTF	Social Progress Trust Fund (of the IDB)
UNCTAD	United Nations Conference on Trade and Development
UNDP	United Nations Development Program

The Inter-American Development Bank

EARLY CONCEPTS

The idea of establishing an inter-American financing institution goes back to the nineteenth century.[1] At the First Inter-American Conference, held during 1889-90, a resolution was adopted recommending the "granting of liberal concessions to facilitate inter-American banking, and especially such as may be necessary for the establishment of an International American Bank, with branches, or agencies, in the several countries represented in this Conference."[2] The ideas underlying this proposal had little in common with those that ultimately led to the establishment of the Inter-American Development Bank (IDB) in 1959.

The principal objective at the first conference was to strengthen the banking links between the United States and the Latin American countries. While the Latin American participants in the conference saw the proposal as a means of reducing Latin American dependence on European banks, the U.S. objective was to capture the financial income that had previously gone to Britain, as well as to extend U.S. influence in the hemisphere.[3] The U.S. Government was, however, unable to prevail over antimonopoly sentiment in Congress.

During the next forty years, U.S. banking activity in Latin America expanded considerably, but attempts to revive the idea of a single inter-American bank failed repeatedly because of continuing opposition to monopolistic aspects of the proposal, as well as concern at the obvious danger that a government-sponsored institution might interfere with, or tend to take over, activities of the private banking community.[4]

In the 1930s, the idea emerged again in a somewhat different form as a result of a proposal by Mexico at the Seventh Inter-American Conference, held in Montevideo in December, 1933, to set up an institution along the lines of a continental central bank to encourage the flow of capital within the region and to help restore monetary stability. Little was done to develop these ideas until the outbreak of World War II in September, 1939, which had the effect of reviving Latin American interest and activity along these lines.

In February, 1940, the Inter-American Economic and Financial Consultative Committee reached agreement on draft statutes for an inter-American bank that was to have the combined functions of a central bank, a commercial bank, and an investment bank. In May, 1940, the convention embodying the draft charter was signed by nine countries including the United States--more than enough to bring the bank into operation. The convention was, however, ratified only by Mexico, and, although it received the support of President Franklin D. Roosevelt and Under-Secretary of State Adolph A. Berle, the U.S. Congress took no action on the matter. Once the United States became involved in World War II, it was, of course, difficult to obtain serious consideration of a question of this sort.

The idea of a regional financing institution did not re-emerge during the first phase of the postwar period. The establishment of the United Nations and specialized agencies, including the International Monetary Fund (IMF) and the International Bank for Reconstruction and Development (IBRD, or World Bank),

reflected a broader international approach to the
world's problems. Moreover, out of the forty-four
countries participating at the Bretton Woods Conference in 1944, no less than nineteen were Latin American, so that Latin America had reason to hope that
its financial needs would receive due attention.

These expectations were disappointed, however,
when it became clear that the efforts made for the
reconstruction of Europe, notably through the Marshall
Plan, were not to be accompanied by a comparable flow
of resources to the developing countries. At the
Ninth Inter-American Conference at Bogotá in 1948,
Mexico and Peru presented proposals for the creation
of an inter-American bank, while Venezuela suggested
the establishment of an inter-American development
corporation. (The Mexican draft noted that "the
IBRD is giving preference to the reconstruction of
devastated countries and that the economic aid that
it can give the American republics for development
has thus far been inadequate, owing variously to the
limitation on its resources, the origin of these resources, and the standards applied to its operations."[5]) The conference approved a resolution calling for a study of these proposals, but the situation
had not yet matured to the point at which ideas along
these lines could achieve sufficient support in the
United States, and the matter was temporarily dropped
early in 1950.

The Tenth Inter-American Conference held in Caracas in March, 1954, did not itself take up the
question of a regional financing institution, but
decided to convene a special meeting of Ministers of
Finance or of Economy for this purpose later in the
year and to seek the cooperation of the Economic Commission for Latin America (ECLA) in preparing for the
meeting.

The Secretariat of ECLA, under the guidance of
Raúl Prebisch, thereupon prepared a report that
pointed out that, from 1950 to 1953, the annual net
inflow of resources into Latin America had averaged
only $421.7 million, of which $342.5 million consisted
of private capital. Only $79.2 million had been made

available by the World Bank and the U.S. Export-
Import Bank (EXIMBANK), taken together, for investment
largely in transportation and power; and this amount
represented barely 3 per cent of aggregate public investment in Latin America, whereas, in the past, the
external contribution to such investment in Latin
America had been proportionally much greater.[6]

The report therefore called for a total volume
of U.S. capital investment in Latin America of at
least $1 billion a year from 1955 to 1957.[7] Since
it could not be expected that private capital would
supply much more than 30-35 per cent of this total,
the report suggested the need for a major increase
in the flow of resources from international lending
institutions.

One obstacle to such an increase was that the
World Bank was unable, under its Articles of Agreement, to lend to private enterprise without government
guarantee. Governments, however, were not very keen
on facing all the difficulties involved in guaranteeing loans to private enterprise; and private entrepreneurs were themselves anxious to avoid government
interference in their affairs. It therefore seemed
necessary, as ECLA saw it, either to set up an international finance corporation as an affiliate of the
World Bank, to expand the operations of EXIMBANK, or
to set up a new inter-American fund to which contributions would be made by the Latin American countries
and, predominantly, by the United States.

It was estimated that such a fund, which should
concentrate on industrial credit operations, would
need initial resources of $50-100 million a year.
Additional resources would be required if the new
fund were to operate also in the field of agriculture,
for which a strong case could be made; however, advantages were seen in having the World Bank enlarge
its agricultural operations so that the inter-American
fund could specialize in industrial credit.[8]

A distinguished group of Latin American experts
was then convened by Prebisch to prepare recommendations for the special economic conference that was

to be held at the ministerial level at the end of
1954 at Quitandinha (Rio de Janeiro). The caliber
of the group may be judged by the subsequent careers
of two of its members; its chairman, Eduardo Frei
Montalva, later became President of Chile, and its
rapporteur, Carlos Lleras Restrepo, became President
of Colombia.

The group agreed with the ECLA Secretariat that
a provisional foreign investment target of $1 billion
a year would be appropriate in terms of Latin America's absorptive capacity and that, given the probable
inflow of private capital, $650-700 million would
probably have to be provided by international credit
institutions. They also approved the proposal for
the establishment of an inter-American fund "to support private enterprise in our countries."[9]

The group recognized that the new activities
that they envisaged--providing assistance to Latin
American industry, agriculture, and mining--could,
in principle, be undertaken by existing agencies,
such as the World Bank and EXIMBANK, but that these
agencies would, in any event, have to develop new
machinery for this purpose, since they had not thus
far engaged in such activities:

> Thus it is not a question of deciding
> whether to create a new organization, since
> this would have to be done in any case, but
> rather whether it should operate in an inde-
> pendent manner. Many practical reasons
> favor this latter solution, principally the
> degree of specialization and the knowledge
> of local conditions that would be indispens-
> able for handling this special type of
> credit to industrial, agricultural or mining
> concerns. This would be true despite the
> fact that the new agency would generally
> operate through the banking systems of our
> countries, and through their financing or
> development institutions.[10]

In order to permit lending operations of $50-100
million annually, the group proposed that the fund

have $250 million capital, half to be contributed by
the United States and half by the Latin American
countries. Only 20 per cent of this amount would be
paid into the fund, and additional resources would
be obtained by an annual U.S. contribution of $50
million and by selling bonds on capital markets guaranteed by the fund's callable capital, as in the
case of the World Bank.

In addition, interest rates charged on loans
would be similar to those levied by the World Bank
and EXIMBANK. The fund would have important technical-assistance functions, to ensure the effective
transfer of technology; and it should be located in
New York, because of the facilities available there
for contacts with U.S. financial and business concerns.[11]

A third report submitted to the Quitandinha
Conference was commissioned by the Organization of
American States (OAS) and prepared by Raymond F.
Mikesell. Mikesell reached the conclusion that Latin
America had the potential capacity to absorb external
capital in amounts several times the current level
and could make effective use of an inflow of as much
as $2 billion a year or more. He pointed out that
such an expansion could be achieved by increasing
the lending authority of EXIMBANK or the World Bank.

He noted, however, that the American states
might decide, for a variety of reasons, to channel
the additional resources through a newly created
inter-American bank. For example, such a bank might
help to alleviate the shortage of personnel for processing loans and providing technical assistance in
the preparation of projects--a shortage that had
been handicapping existing institutions. It might
also be especially effective in regional development
planning and the financing of regional projects.[12]

Regarding the need to provide facilities for
making loan capital available to Latin American private enterprise without government guarantee, Mikesell believed that this could be done either by the
proposed international finance corporation, to be

affiliated with the World Bank, or by an inter-American equivalent; but he went further, by recommending
that the selected institution should also be authorized to provide equity capital.[13]

At the Quitandinha Conference itself, held from
November 22 to December 2, 1954, several proposals
for the creation of an inter-American development
bank were put forward. The most noteworthy of these
proposals was the one advanced by Chile and supported
by Colombia, Costa Rica, Ecuador, and Haiti; in view
of the reluctance of the United States to participate
in a regional bank, the Chilean delegation suggested
that the main resources of such a bank could be provided by the Latin American countries themselves.

The conference, in a resolution on which the
United States and Peru abstained, called for the con-
vening of a committee of experts consisting of the
representatives of central banks of nine Latin American countries and of the ECLA Secretariat to make
specific proposals to the OAS for the creation of a
regional financing institution. The committee duly
met in Santiago from February to April, 1955, and
drew up a draft agreement.

THE SANTIAGO DRAFT

The "Santiago Draft" provided for the establishment of an inter-American development bank to supplement the efforts of existing lending agencies. The
primary objective of the bank, according to the
draft, would be to promote the economic development
of its member countries by investing in the creation
or expansion of enterprises, operations, and services,
whether public, private, or mixed. It would finance
not only productive projects in the traditional sense
but also social-overhead projects, such as roads,
sanitation, and water supply, as well as the local
costs of projects.

The bank would also grant lines of credit in
support of broad development programs, with the understanding that drawings against such credits would be

authorized only as individual projects included in
the respective programs were duly approved. Special
emphasis was placed on guarantee operations by the
bank in support of efforts by public or private entities to borrow in capital markets. The bank's
capital was to be set at $200 million, half of which
was to be paid in, with the remainder intended to
guarantee obligations that it issued. The bank would
borrow from other institutions and from capital markets, would accept deposits, and would sell participations in its portfolio.

Although the United States did not take part in
the work on the Santiago Draft and had thus far rejected any idea of establishing a regional development bank, it was assumed that the United States
would be willing, in due course, to put up one-third
of the subscribed capital, the remainder being furnished by the Latin American countries themselves.
Quotas were to be determined on the basis of quotas
in the IMF, with Argentina (then a nonmember of the
IMF) assigned a quota equal to that of Brazil. Paid-in
capital would consist of gold or dollars.

Although the bank would place its main emphasis
on medium-term lending (with maturities of three to
eight years), it would also be able to provide short-
term loans for financing imports of equipment and the
execution of projects not requiring longer maturities.
It would likewise give long-term loans in appropriate
cases. Short-term loans, because of their possible
balance-of-payments implications, would be granted
only to entities duly authorized by governments or
central banks to accept such loans. Medium- and
long-term loans would be advanced to public, private,
or mixed institutions. Government guarantees would
not be needed, but loans would not be granted in
cases where the governments concerned raised objec-
tions. Loans would not be tied to exports from particular countries.

The bank's decisions would be subject to a system of weighted voting similar to that employed in
the IMF and the World Bank, but no member would hold
more than one-third of the total voting power. The

bank would be administered by a president and six
directors. The president would be elected by not
less than two-thirds of the members and two-thirds
of the votes. One director would be nominated by
the country with the largest number of votes--the
United States--and the remaining directors would be
elected under a special procedure.

The draft statutes described above were duly
submitted to the Inter-American Economic and Social
Council in June, 1955, which, in turn, forwarded them
to governments for consideration and comment. The
replies gave little encouragement to the supporters
of the idea of a regional development bank. Only
nine countries signified approval of the draft statutes in principle, two gave qualified replies, and
three (including the United States) registered opposition. The remaining seven countries--including
three of those that had supplied experts to the drafting committee--gave no answer at all.[14]

It is likely that the divided response of the
Latin American countries reflected skepticism about
whether the bank would be viable if the United States
refused to join and if, as a result, the bank were
unable to gain access to the U.S. capital market.
In any event, the failure to obtain the support of
at least fourteen countries subscribing at least 50
per cent of the authorized capital--the condition
laid down by the draft statutes--meant that the statutes had to be shelved.

The deadlock persisted during a whole series of
inter-American meetings in the course of 1956 and
1957. The Economic Conference of the OAS held in
Buenos Aires in August and September, 1957, noted
that views were still divided about how best to channel external resources to Latin America, with some
countries favoring the use of existing agencies and
others advocating the establishment of a new regional
financing institution. The conference nevertheless
called for a continuation of studies of such an institution by the Inter-American Economic and Social
Council, which was asked to convene a special inter-
governmental committee for this purpose.

The conference further expressed appreciation
of the "progress" made by the international financial
institutions since Quitandinha, but reaffirmed the
request made to the World Bank at that time to consider financing the local costs of projects, as well
as the opening of lines of credit for assisting development programs--recommendations that the World
Bank had not thus far implemented.[15]

A European development with obvious implications
for the western hemisphere was the establishment of
the European Development Fund (EDF), under the Treaty
of Rome in 1957, in order to provide assistance to
the African nations and other countries associated
with the European Economic Community (EEC). If the
EEC was prepared to make financial assistance available on a regional basis to African countries, it
was natural for the Latin American countries to ask
why the United States should not consider a similar
approach to the Latin American region.

OPERATION PAN AMERICA

A turning point in the negotiations for an inter-
American bank was reached in 1958. The growing sentiment in Latin America that the United States was
neglecting the needs of its closest neighbors was
expressed with particular force during the visit of
Vice-President Richard M. Nixon to the region early
in that year. Although the demonstrations that took
place in a number of capitals were the work of an
activist minority, it was recognized that dissatis-
faction in Latin America had become widespread and
acute.

The reception given to the U.S. Vice-President
prompted Brazilian President Juscelino Kubitschek to
address an important message to President Dwight D.
Eisenhower on May 28, 1958. After deploring the
"aggressions and vexations undergone by Vice-President
Nixon during his recent visit to countries in Latin
America," President Kubitschek expressed the view
that

the hour has come for us to undertake jointly
a thorough review of the policy of mutual
understanding on this Hemisphere and to conduct a comprehensive reappraisal of the pro-
ceedings already in motion for the further-
ance of Pan American ideals in all their
aspects and implications. . . . It is hoped
that the unpleasant memory of the ordeal
undergone by Vice-President Nixon will be
effaced by the results of earnest efforts
towards creating something deeper and more
durable for the defense and preservation of
our common destiny.[16]

In his reply, dated June 5, 1958, President Eisenhower
said that

to my mind you have described accurately
both the existing situation and the desirability of corrective action . . . it seems
to me that our two Governments should con-
sult together as soon as possible with a
view to approaching other members of the
Pan American community, and starting promptly
on measures that would produce throughout
the continent a reaffirmation of devotion to
Pan Americanism, and better planning in promoting the common interests and welfare of
our several countries.[17]

The two governments quickly reached agreement on the
steps to be taken, as the result of a visit by Secretary of State John Foster Dulles to Rio de Janeiro
on August 4.

On August 12, 1958, the Brazilian Government
submitted an aide-mémoire to all members of the OAS,
setting out the fundamental objectives of Operation
Pan America. What was sought was a "reorientation
of hemispheric policy, intended to place Latin America, by a process of full appraisement, in a position
to participate more effectively in the defense of
the West" and thereby contribute to "preservation of
the democratic system, based on political and religious

freedom and on respect for private ownership and free enterprise, and the defense of all areas that concern the security of the free world."

The basic economic concept of Operation Pan America was that "the more rapid development of Latin America's economic strength will result in a growing sense of vitality and will enable it to increase its contribution to the defense of the West."[18] Thus, the success of Operation Pan America in persuading the United States to reconsider Latin American development needs was due to the manner in which it linked political, military, and economic objectives. The aide-mémoire argued that the

> struggle for democracy becomes identified
> with the struggle against stagnation and
> underdevelopment . . . the battle of the
> West is the battle for development. Ma-
> terialist ideologies feed upon the poverty
> and misery that give rise to them in the
> first place; to combat these factors is the
> only sure way to combat those ideologies.[19]

Brazil therefore proposed a high-level meeting to adopt a plan of action for achieving Pan American unity. It was suggested that preparations for this meeting should be made by a Committee of Twenty-one of the OAS, which should consider, inter alia, the question of an "increase in the volume and an easing of the terms of loans made by international public credit agencies, or the creation of inter-American financing institutions organized with the same objective in mind."[20]

While these events were taking place in Latin America, serious tensions and conflicts were building up in the Middle East. In June, 1958, following allegations by Lebanon of intervention by the United Arab Republic in its internal affairs, the U.N. Security Council decided to send observers to Lebanon; and, on July 15, at the urgent request of the President of Lebanon, the United States sent troops to that country. As part of an effort to bring greater tranquillity to the area, President Eisenhower decided

to propose to the U.N. General Assembly, on August
13, 1958, the establishment of an "Arab development
institution on a regional basis," with functions very
similar to those suggested by Latin American countries
for an inter-American development bank.

Its objective would be to accelerate progress
in such fields as industry, agriculture, water supply,
health, and education. The requisite financial resources would be contributed by the United States,
the Arab countries, and other nations; and the institution would attract international capital, both
public and private. It would be administered by the
Arab states themselves.[21]

The United States recognized that it could
scarcely make a proposal along these lines for the
Middle East without conceding the long-standing Latin
American request for a regional development bank as
well. Indeed, Secretary of the Treasury Robert B.
Anderson strongly insisted that priority should be
given to the idea of an inter-American bank, and this
recommendation was accepted by President Eisenhower.

As a result, one day before the President's
statement to the General Assembly, Under-Secretary
of State C. Douglas Dillon announced at a special
session of the Inter-American Economic and Social
Council, on August 12, 1958, that the United States
was ready to "consider the establishment of an inter-
American regional development institution which would
receive support from all its member countries."[22]

This statement prepared the way for the establishment of a negotiating committee to draw up an
agreement for the creation of an inter-American development bank. The committee began its work in
January, 1959, and completed it in April of that year.
The agreement was signed in April, 1959, and entered
into force on December 30, 1959, the requisite number
of ratifications having been submitted. The first
meeting of the Board of Governors of the IDB was held
in February, 1960, and the President and the first
Board of Executive Directors were elected. The Bank
officially began its operations on October 1, 1960,
and made its first loan in February, 1961.

THE LATIN AMERICAN CASE
FOR A REGIONAL BANK

The most fundamental element in the Latin American case for a regional development bank was that such
an institution was an indispensable part of the inter-
American system. There was a long tradition of political and economic cooperation among the countries
belonging to this system, and the OAS, with its various subsidiary organs in specialized fields, was a
manifestation of the general desire for a special
relationship among the countries of the hemisphere.
It was felt that the smooth conduct of inter-American
relations depended upon a satisfactory rate of economic and social progress throughout the region and
that a regional development bank was therefore required to ensure that external financial needs could
be met.

The Latin American countries were also beginning
to see the need for a lending institution that would
specialize in the problems of Latin America and devote its entire attention to their particular needs.
As they saw it, a regional bank would be able to make
itself more familiar with, and responsive to, local
conditions in the individual countries with which it
was dealing.

As noted earlier, the Latin American countries
had accounted for nearly one-half of the original
membership of the World Bank. As time went on, however, more and more of the colonial dependencies
achieved independence and qualified for World Bank
membership. In these circumstances, the field of
operations of the World Bank was enormously extended,
and the possibilities for concentrating on the problems of any one region were correspondingly reduced.
Moreover, it could be held that many of the new members of the World Bank were at a much earlier level
of development and at a lower level of income than
were the Latin American countries and were therefore
entitled to some priority.

Particularly important in the campaign for a
regional development bank was the growing sense

of regional solidarity in Latin America. The very
same forces that were pressing for the establishment
of the bank were also prompting the Latin American
countries to strengthen their cooperation with one
another through schemes of regional integration. It
is no accident that the founding of the IDB coincided
closely in time with the signing of the Treaty of
Montevideo, which provided for the establishment of
the Latin American Free Trade Association (LAFTA),
and with the Treaty of Managua, which set up the Central American Common Market (CACM).

Also, it was natural that one of the principal
functions of the IDB specified in the basic agreement
setting it up was

> to cooperate with the member countries to
> orient their development policies toward a
> better utilization of their resources, in
> a manner consistent with the objectives of
> making their economies more complementary
> and of fostering the orderly growth of their
> foreign trade.[23]

A major consideration in the proposal for a regional development bank for Latin America was the
expectation that this would encourage a larger flow
of financial resources to Latin American countries.
Bilateral flows of assistance to Latin America during
the 1950s had averaged less than $200 million a year,
whereas multilateral flows had averaged $50-60 million
a year. During the early 1950s, many Latin American
countries had been able to finance a high level of
import requirements because export prices for coffee
and certain other primary products had been very favorable, and some of these countries had also been
able to make use of foreign-exchange resources ac-
cumulated during World War II and early postwar periods, when exports had been buoyant and imports had
been difficult to obtain.

During the second half of the 1950s, however,
the special factors that had supported Latin American
import capacity during the early postwar period dis-
appeared, and Latin America was particularly hard
hit by declines in the prices of primary products

following the end of the Korean War and, particularly, by the drop in coffee prices after 1954. In these circumstances, the Latin American countries began pressing much more strongly than before for an expansion of the inflow of capital.

Another factor, and a powerful one, was the desire of the Latin American countries to play a major role in the administration of assistance programs for the region. The example of the Marshall Plan had shown the benefits that could be derived if aid-receiving countries were made responsible for the administration and distribution of funds provided.

Although it was recognized that the United States, as the supplier of capital, would be entitled to play a decisive role in the running of any regional bank that might be established, it was felt that it would nevertheless be possible for the bank to be staffed largely from Latin America and would thereby enable the Latin American countries to participate in the running of the aid program in a much more direct sense than was possible in the World Bank. The Marshall Plan precedent was followed not only with respect to the establishment of the IDB but, also, in the subsequent creation of the Inter-American Committee for the Alliance for Progress (CIAP), with which the IDB cooperates closely, as will be shown later.

The Latin American countries were also anxious to enlist the cooperation of a multilateral development agency that would take strong initiatives in promoting and stimulating the economic and social growth of the region. The World Bank of the mid-1950s was not yet the vigorous development institution that it was to become later on; it was still very much under the influence of the ideas of Bretton Woods.

As conceived at Bretton Woods, the World Bank was viewed primarily as a means for restoring the flow of private capital from the industrial countries to the rest of the world, a flow that had ceased during the 1930s as a result of the many defaults of the depression years and that seemed unlikely to be

resumed in the postwar period unless special steps
were taken to restore confidence. The method chosen
was to establish a solidly based international bank,
carrying the joint backing of all member countries,
and to give it the responsibility for borrowing private capital on the security afforded by its inter-
governmental backing and for relending the proceeds
to finance suitable projects in member countries.

Although this was the method of operation ultimately adopted by the World Bank, it is of interest
to recall the original approach of its founders, who
envisaged narrow limits for World Bank activity.
Assistant Secretary of State Dean Acheson's testimony
before Congress in April, 1945, made it clear that,
as originally conceived, the main function of the
World Bank was to "investigate the soundness of the
projects for which capital is desired and, if [the
World Bank] agrees they are sound, it will guarantee
loans made by private banks."[24] The ability of the
World Bank to make direct loans out of its own resources was referred to by Acheson only as an after-
thought, in parentheses, and it was suggested that
such direct loans would be given by the World Bank
only when private capital was not available.

The same line of thinking was reflected by a
U.S. Treasury representative in his testimony before
Congress:

> We hope that the American investor will un-
> dertake many of the loans so that there will
> be little business for the Bank: in fact,
> the Bank would be most welcome if it did no
> business because that would indicate that
> the American investor is willing to make
> loans at reasonable rates and that condi-
> tions abroad were such as to give the indi-
> vidual investor confidence in such loans.[25]

The general approach was summed up by Secretary of
the Treasury Henry Morgenthau as follows:

> The operation of the Bank would offer the
> best protection the American investor has

ever enjoyed in the field of foreign finance.
The facilities of the Bank are to be such
that the private American purchaser of foreign bonds will know that impartial experts
have considered the purpose of the loan
sound. If the Bank's own money goes into
floating the issue, the loan will also be
guaranteed by the borrowing country and by
all the resources of the Bank as derived
from 44 member nations. People who bought
certain foreign bonds during the twenties
will realize how great a boon this can be.[26]

In practice, it was found more effective for the
World Bank to lend directly out of its own resources,
rather than to guarantee loans made by others. But
it remained true, in the early years, that the principal function of the World Bank was to provide "a
safe bridge over which private capital could move
into the international field."[27] The emphasis was
thus upon providing security for the ultimate lender--
private capital--at least as much as on promoting the
development of potential borrowers; and it was inevitable that the constraints imposed by the first
of these concerns should affect the manner in which
the second was handled--as they still do, to some
extent, even now, as will be seen subsequently. (See
Chapters 3 and 9, below.)

It was not yet considered to be the task of the
World Bank to view the development problems of its
members in a broad framework and to take active steps
to assist them in dealing with those problems, including, where necessary, taking the initiative in
developing new projects. Still less was it the function of the World Bank to provide general support
for well-conceived development programs.

Least of all was it in a position to concern itself with the social needs of the developing countries
or with projects that, although essential in the development process, could not yield measurable returns
in the usual banking sense. Latin American countries,
therefore, wished to see the establishment of a new
institution that would be able to innovate with

respect to its lending policies and to attend to the
needs of agriculture, industry, urban development--
including low-income housing--pure water supplies,
health and sanitation, and education.

Some of the Latin American countries were also
greatly concerned about the difficulties encountered
in meeting the standards required by the World Bank
and other agencies for project preparation. This
matter was brought up forcefully at meetings of the
Inter-American Committee of Presidential Representatives held in 1956-57. One of the functions envisaged
for a regional development bank was that it would
maintain close contact with the process of planning
and project preparation in each of its member countries, assisting, where necessary, prospective borrowers in drawing up projects in the manner required
and informing them as to the various steps and commitments that would be required of them.[28]

A further consideration was that many of the
Latin American countries were in acute balance-of-
payments difficulties, aggravated by the weakening of
demand for their exports. Consequently, there appeared to be a strong case for easing the terms of
borrowing, especially for the less developed among
them. It is true that this did not necessarily call
for the establishment of a regional bank, since suitable facilities could have been provided within the
World Bank--as, indeed, they later were. But during
most of the period of the 1950s, when the possible
establishment of a Latin American regional bank had
been under discussion, there had been resistance to
the idea that development loans on easy terms might
be provided within the World Bank framework, on the
grounds that this might damage the World Bank's
standing in the capital markets on which it depended
for the success of its bond flotations. As far back
as 1949, John J. McCloy, then President of the World
Bank, had told the U.N. Economic and Employment Commission that he would not be a party to the creation
of a "bargain basement" within the World Bank.

Some observers saw dangers in an overcentraliza-
tion of development lending. Although there is much

to be said for a measure of central coordination in
the aid-giving process, a completely monolithic and
monopolistic aid structure would be undesirable not
only from the standpoint of borrowers but, also, from
that of lenders, as will be argued subsequently. The
borrowing countries would clearly be at a disadvantage
if they always had to face a single institution with
a single set of ideas, however worthy.

In addition, large institutions are always in
danger of becoming somewhat bureaucratic and set in
their ways, and the criteria that they apply may
sometimes tend to become matters more of routine and
precedent than of careful analysis. This is particularly true of a field, such as economic development,
in which there are unfortunately few objective standards that can be applied rigorously. Latin American
countries, therefore, saw advantages in some diversification of the multilateral sources of funds.

It does not, of course, necessarily follow that
errors will be avoided simply because there are two
or more agencies ready to entertain applications rather than only one. On the whole, the international
lending agencies tend to march roughly in step with
one another, and major divergencies in policy tend
to be discouraged by the aid-giving countries. Nevertheless, it was the hope and expectation of the
Latin American countries that the existence of more
than one agency to which they could turn might provide some additional assurance that reasonable requests would not be turned down for insufficient
reasons.

They believed that there was likely to be a better chance that their case would be heard fairly if
they could deal with two or more institutions rather
than one. Moreover, although rivalry between two or
more institutions operating in the same or similar
fields is often seen as a form of waste, it may also
have its positive side in spurring them all to greater
efforts and more receptive attitudes. There are indications that Latin American expectations were not
wholly misplaced on this score, since, particularly
in recent years, the World Bank and the IDB both have

expanded their financing of Latin American development
and have gone out into the field actively in the
search for suitable projects.

Finally, the establishment of the IDB may be regarded as one of the responses to the long campaign
by the developing countries as a whole to establish
a Capital Development Fund within the United Nations.
That campaign had begun during the early 1950s, following the submission of a report, in 1951, by a
special group of experts.[29]

The campaign had sought to create an institution
that would be subject to the control of the United
Nations, with its one-country/one-vote system, on the
grounds that such an agency would be much more responsive to the needs of developing countries than was
the World Bank, which was dominated by the heavily
preponderant voting power of the major industrial
countries.

As has already been pointed out, although this
campaign did not succeed in achieving its principal
objective, it did elicit a number of important concessions from the industrial countries. In particular, the expansion of the resources of the IMF and
of the IBRD, the enlargement of the U.N. technical-
assistance program, including the establishment of
the U.N. Special Fund and the creation of the IDB,
the International Development Association (IDA), and
the International Finance Corporation (IFC), may all
be traced in some degree to the desire of the developed countries to make a response to developing-coun-
try pressures without conceding a Capital Development
Fund within the United Nations.[30]

THE U.S. RESPONSE

The United States resisted the pressure for a
regional development bank for Latin America, not acceding to the request of the Latin American countries
until 1958. Although the United States continued to
regard western hemisphere unity and cooperation as a
key element in its foreign policy, its standing as a

world power made it necessary to consider very care-
fully any request for special treatment that might
have repercussions on its relationships with the rest
of the world.

Ever since the 1920s, the trade policy of the
United States had been based on the principle of non-
discrimination, and the United States sought, during
and after World War II, to enlist the agreement of
the European colonial powers, particularly the United
Kingdom and France, to the elimination of their dis-
criminatory trade ties with the dependent territories.
It was therefore a matter for consideration whether
special arrangements for financial aid to Latin America might be regarded as inconsistent with the broader
economic policies that the United States had been
pursuing over several decades.

There was a danger that any move by the United
States to concentrate its assistance upon Latin America alone might be interpreted by the rest of the
world as an acceptance of the prewar spheres-of-
influence policies that the United States had been
trying to persuade its allies to reject. Thus, any
decision to increase the flow of resources to Latin
America might have to be accompanied by a corresponding willingness to increase the volume of assistance
to Africa and Asia as well, and for this the United
States was not yet ready.

There were also considerable advantages, within
limits, in the centralization of multilateral assistance in a single institution. For example, there
are economies of scale--unit overhead expenses are
likely to be lower, up to a certain point, the larger
is the program that has to be administered. At the
same time, the task of officials in aid-receiving
countries, where skilled administrative manpower is
scarce, is bound to be simpler the smaller is the
number of external financial agencies with which they
have to deal.

There was also much to be gained from assembling
worldwide experience in development lending in a
single center. Such a central institution would be

able to compare and contrast successful projects in
some areas with failures in others and to draw useful
conclusions regarding the best way of approaching
particular types of projects under various kinds of
local conditions. Provided that such an institution
could solve the problem of internal coordination, its
worldwide scope would be an immense asset in accumulating and interpreting development experience.

It is probably also easier to secure a rational
basis for burden-sharing among donors and an equitable
system of distribution of loans among recipients
within a single institution than it is in a whole complex of global and regional institutions. No lending
country is likely to agree that its share in contributions to, say, the World Bank Group ought to be
larger because it is not a member of--and, therefore,
does not contribute to--one or more of the regional
banks to which other lending countries belong.

Similarly, it has been shown repeatedly that
there is no valid basis for the existing pattern of
distribution of assistance among the developing countries that results from the haphazard aggregation of
grants and loans by the national and international
agencies combined.[31]

In the case of an inter-American bank, it was
apparent that the great bulk of resources, apart from
the limited funds that the Latin American countries
themselves would be able to put up, would have to
come from the United States. Potential European con-
tributors were not members of the inter-American system, and it was realized that it might be difficult
to enlist their participation in a regional development bank that was clearly designed to support a
political and economic alliance to which they did not
belong.

Moreover, the very same factors that prompted
the Latin American countries to think that their influence would be greater in a regional bank than it
was in the World Bank were persuasive in deterring
the United States from acceding to the proposal. It
was easy to see that, no matter what its voting power

in a regional bank might be, the United States would
have to expect to face the political and financial
consequences of being in a minority of one whenever
confronted by a united stand on any particular issue
by the Latin American countries as a group.

Although the experience of the Marshall Plan had
clearly demonstrated the advantages of having recipient countries participate in the running of an aid
program, there were doubts in the United States about
the ability of the Latin American countries to provide
staff for a regional development bank with the skills
in financial management and appraisal that were
needed. There was a fear that it might prove exceed-
ingly difficult to recruit staff and top management
that would run the bank on sufficiently orthodox lines
to convince potential investors that they could safely
entrust their money to it.

As far as the idea of creating an inter-American
bank to make direct loans to private enterprise was
concerned, the U.S. view was that such a bank would
compete with private credit institutions or would
duplicate the facilities offered by EXIMBANK. The
United States therefore indicated its willingness to
expand the activities of EXIMBANK in order to make
it more responsive to Latin American requirements.

Basic to the U.S. approach was the belief that
"only private enterprise is equal to the task of
developing the huge resources of this vast hemisphere."[32] The bulk of the external resource requirements of Latin America should therefore be met by
private foreign investment. Only insofar as private
capital was not available for essential projects
should there be recourse to public funds, and all
such requirements could be met by the World Bank or
EXIMBANK, without any need for setting up a new
institution.

Nevertheless, the United States recognized that
there was an important defect in the Articles of
Agreement of the World Bank insofar as they precluded
loans to private enterprise without government guarantee. Since amendment of the Articles of Agreement was

regarded as an excessively formidable task, requiring
parliamentary sanction in the member countries, it
was decided to graft a new entity onto the World Bank
in the form of the IFC.

As George M. Humphrey, U.S. Secretary of the
Treasury, told the Quitandinha Conference:

> If the International Finance Corporation is
> established, we shall then have three major
> financial institutions to help promote eco-
> nomic development. We shall have the Export-
> Import Bank that has had a long history of
> useful work in Latin America and whose ac-
> tivities are to be intensified. We shall
> have the International Bank, in which we
> are partners, to help finance basic resource
> development. We shall have an Interna-
> tional Finance Corporation in which we would
> work together to assist and encourage pri-
> vate enterprise.[33]

The Latin American countries did not, however, regard
this as an adequate response to their point of view,
since the IFC, like the World Bank, was to have worldwide scope, whereas they were seeking an institution
that would concentrate on the particular problems of
Latin America. Latin American pressure for a regional
development bank was therefore maintained, despite
the failure of this idea at Quitandinha.

RECONSIDERATION BY THE
UNITED STATES

No official statement exists on the precise reasons for the change that took place in 1958 in the
U.S. position on the establishment of a regional development bank for Latin America. It is therefore
impossible to be certain about which factors were
uppermost in this decision. Undoubtedly, the U.S.
Government must have been impressed by the strength
of feeling in Latin America on this matter. It became increasingly apparent that the broad goals of
the United States in the hemisphere could not be

realized without attending much more closely to the
development needs of the Latin American countries.

The requirements for assistance became particularly acute, as noted previously, following the decline in the prices of primary commodities, especially
coffee, after the end of the Korean War. Latin American spokesmen were continually drawing attention to
the sharp contrast between the vast funds poured out
by the United States for the reconstruction of Western
Europe--a region that already possessed a high standard of living--and the limited resources made available to assist much poorer countries in Latin America
in raising their standards of living to more-tolerable
levels.[34] (Resentment over this situation came to a
head during Vice-President Nixon's visit to Latin
America in 1958, as noted earlier.)

Given the prevailing Latin American mood, thrown
into relief by the reception given to the Vice-President, it must have appeared that the establishment of
a regional development bank would constitute one
rather effective method of channeling the forces of
continental nationalism into productive channels.
The willingness of the Latin American countries to
contribute to a joint effort for the development of
the region must have seemed to be one of the most attractive potential features of a regional bank, fully
in line with the concept of self-help that was being
stressed by the U.S. Government.

These ideas of hemisphere cooperation for development were later to receive more articulated expression in the Alliance for Progress initiated by
President Kennedy. But the foundations for this approach had been laid during the term of office of
President Eisenhower, who, in the Declaration of New-
port in July, 1960, stated it to be the policy of
the United States to cooperate with the countries of
Latin America in enlarged programs of economic and
social development.

Although the establishment of the IDB preceded
the proclamation of the Alliance for Progress, many
of the concepts later applied in connection with the

Alliance were influential, on the U.S. side, in
bringing about acceptance of the IDB. The mood of
the time has been described as follows:

> Washington felt a genuine sense of urgency.
> It was feared that discontent was growing
> fast in Latin America, especially in the
> burgeoning cities and among campesinos and
> workers, and that radical political move-
> ments would gain strength. It was expected
> that Castro's example might soon be followed
> elsewhere in the hemisphere. It was said
> that in Latin America it was "one minute to
> midnight," that either "evolution or revo-
> lution" would soon occur there, and that
> only U.S. support for far-reaching reforms
> could stave off shattering violence. . . .
> It was assumed that economic growth, social
> equity, political stability and constitu-
> tional democracy all went hand in hand and
> could therefore be advanced simultaneously
> in Latin America. All these objectives were
> also thought to be compatible with protect-
> ing various U.S. interests in the hemisphere,
> including national security and private
> U.S. investments. . . . A switch in Wash-
> ington's approach from the studied disin-
> terest of the 1950s to active encouragement
> of Latin American development was expected
> to produce major gains. Finally, it was
> believed that the American public, and par-
> ticularly the Congress and various élite
> groups, were particularly concerned about
> Latin America and would willingly support
> a sustained commitment of U.S. economic as-
> sistance for the area.[35]

A U.S. decision to step up the flow of resources
to Latin America could, of course, have been implemented through the World Bank, rather than through
the creation of an inter-American development bank;
but, even though this would not have harnessed, to
the same extent, the growing movement for hemisphere
cooperation for development and the forces of continental nationalism in Latin America, advantages may

also have been seen in the opportunity for institutional diversification.

Although there is a certain simplicity and economy in concentrating the multilateral aid relationship in one channel, there are also dangers in such
concentration, especially if a particular agency were
to expand to the point at which it might become difficult for even the largest countries to control it.
When the lending countries accepted the establishment
of the regional development banks,[36] they were fully
aware that the purposes of these new agencies would,
to some extent, overlap with those of the World Bank.

These countries were prepared, however, to see
a certain pluralism in multilateral aid policies and
practices introduced in the interest of creating institutions that would specialize in the problems of
particular areas and in order to give the developing
countries concerned a greater sense of participation
and identification. They were able to accept the
idea that any loss of economy or administrative simplicity that might result from a certain amount of
institutional duplication might well be counterbal-
anced by significant advantages in other ways.

In any event, the position of the United States
on the establishment of the IDB was summed up in a
message to Congress from President Eisenhower in the
following terms:

I am strongly of the opinion that, because
of the following general policy considerations, the United States should support the
creation of this Bank for Latin America:

(1)   The special relationship, historical,
      political and economic, between the
      United States and the Latin American
      republics;

(2)   The pressing economic and social prob-
      lems in the area resulting from a
      rapid rate of increase in population
      and widespread desire for improved
      living conditions; and

(3)   The desirability of an institution
       which will specialize in the needs of
       Latin America, which will be supported
       in large part by Latin American re-
       sources and which will give the Latin
       American members a major responsibil-
       ity in determining priorities and au-
       thorizing loans.[37]

The U.S. conception of the Bank was also reflected subsequently in the emphasis placed on the
financing of projects of social development as a
means of distributing the benefits of economic growth
more widely and thereby, it was hoped, reducing tensions in Latin America and promoting political and
social stability. In September, 1960, the Committee
of Twenty-one of the OAS, meeting in Bogotá, proposed
the creation of a special inter-American fund for
social development, to be administered primarily by
the IDB, on the understanding that important reforms
and other measures of self-help would be adopted by
the Latin American countries.[38]

Emphasis on the need for social development was
also a feature of President Kennedy's Alliance for
Progress address of March, 1961, which led to the
Punta del Este Conference held that August. In May,
1961, President Kennedy allocated $394 million to a
Social Progress Trust Fund (SPTF), to be administered
under a trust agreement by the IDB. (The U.S. Government subsequently raised its contribution to the
fund to $525 million.) The key role envisaged for
the IDB in promoting the aims of the Alliance for
Progress was further indicated in the provision made
at the Punta del Este Conference for the IDB to coordinate financial assistance from all sources to individual Latin American countries in implementation
of the objectives of the Alliance. (See Chapter 7,
below.)

NOTES

1. For a complete record of the historical
background of the IDB, see Julius Broide, Banco Interamericano de Desarrollo: Sus Antecedentes y Creación

(Washington, D.C.:   IDB, 1968); and Diego Cordovez
Zegers, El Banco Interamericano de Desarrollo (Santiago de Chile: Editorial Universitaria, 1962).

   2.   U.S., International American Conference,
Reports of Committees and Discussions Thereon, II
(Washington, D.C.:   Government Printing Office, 1890),
875.

   3.   Suzanne W. Gardner and John P. Powelson,
"Regional Banking in the Americas," Inter-American
Economic Affairs, XXIV, 1 (Summer, 1970), 17-18.

   4.   Ibid., pp. 18-19.

   5.   See Cordovez Zegers, El Banco Interamericano
de Desarrollo, p. 26.

   6.   U.N., International Cooperation in a Latin
American Development Policy (U.N. Sales No.
1954.II.G.2), September, 1954, pp. 13-14.

   7.   Ibid., pp. 18-19.

   8.   Ibid., pp. 34-36.

   9.   Ibid., p. 107.

   10. Ibid., p. 108.

   11. Ibid., pp. 131-33.

   12. Raymond F. Mikesell, Foreign Investments in
Latin America (Washington, D.C.:   Pan American Union,
1955), pp. 130-35 and 140.

   13. Ibid., pp. 127-28 and 140.

   14. Those supporting the draft statutes in principle were Chile, Colombia, Costa Rica, Dominican
Republic, Ecuador, El Salvador, Honduras, Mexico,
Panama; those giving qualified replies were Bolivia
and Brazil; and those against were Cuba, Peru, and
the United States.   The members of the committee of
experts had been nominated by Argentina, Brazil,

Chile, Colombia, Costa Rica, Cuba, Haiti, Mexico, Venezuela, and the Executive Secretary of ECLA.

15. The Quitandinha Conference had also recommended that the World Bank furnish loans to deal with cases of temporary balance-of-payments disequilibrium, as well as other types of credit not currently provided by that institution. These recommendations were not repeated at Buenos Aires. The omission of the former no doubt reflected the view that the credits envisaged fell within the sphere of responsibility of the IMF. See also the discussion of balance-of-payments support in Chapter 8, below.

16. Department of State Bulletin, XXXVIII, 1091.

17. Ibid., p. 1090.

18. U.S., Department of State, American Foreign Policy, Current Documents 1958 (Washington, D.C., 1962), pp. 404-5.

19. Ibid.

20. Ibid., p. 408.

21. Department of State Bulletin, XXXIX, 339-40.

22. American Foreign Policy, pp. 408-9.

23. IDB, Agreement Establishing the Inter-American Development Bank (Washington, D.C., April, 1959), Art. I, sec. 2 (a)(iv). [Hereafter referred to as Agreement.]

24. U.S., Congress, House, Committee on Banking and Currency, Hearing on H.R. 2211, Bretton Woods Agreements Act, 79th Cong., 1st sess., 1945, II, 34.

25. Ibid., p. 104.

26. Ibid., p. 6.

27.   IBRD, The World Bank, IDA and IFC: Policies
and Operations (Washington, D.C., April, 1968), P. 4.

28.   Since there seemed to be little prospect,
for the time being, that a regional bank would be
established to carry out these functions, the committee recommended the creation of an ad hoc technical
committee to assist Latin American countries in
studying and preparing bankable projects.   See Broide,
Banco Interamericano de Desarrollo, pp. 99-100.

29.   In a report entitled Measures for the
Economic Development of Underdeveloped Countries
(U.N. Sales No. 1951.II.B.2), published in May, 1951,
a group of experts appointed by the Secretary-General
of the United Nations recommended that the United
Nations should establish an International Development
Authority to provide grants-in-aid to developing countries in an amount that should eventually reach a
level of $3 billion a year.

30.   See John J. Hadwen and Johan Kaufman, How
United Nations Decisions Are Made (Leyden: A. W.
Sythof, 1961), p. 114.

31.   See, for example, the following statement
by the Chairman of the Development Assistance Committee (DAC):   "It is argued--and rightly--that the
present geographical pattern of aid flows is not a
wholly rational one, at least from the standpoint of
promoting development, both in the sense that it is
not based upon common objective developmental criteria and that the sum of bilateral and multilateral
donor flows does not always even out inequities
arising from decisions by individual donors."   OECD,
Development Assistance, 1969 Review, Report by Edwin
M. Martin, Chairman of DAC (Paris, December, 1969),
p. 157.

32.   See statement of Henry F. Holland, Assistant
Secretary of State for Inter-American Affairs, to
the Pan American Society of the United States on
October 27, 1954, in Department of State Bulletin,
XXXI, 627.

33. Statement of George M. Humphrey, Secretary
of the Treasury, to the Meeting of Ministers of Finance or of Economy at Quitandinha, Brazil, on November 23, 1954, in Department of State Bulletin, XXXI,
868.

34. No program of assistance (as distinct from
EXIMBANK financing) was provided to Latin America by
the United States prior to fiscal year 1951. In fiscal year 1953, Latin America received $21 million
from the United States, as against Europe's one and
one-quarter billion dollars. Not until fiscal year
1959, just prior to the establishment of the IDB,
did total U.S. loans and grants to Latin America exceed an annual rate of $100 million.

35. Abraham F. Lowenthal, "Alliance Rhetoric
Versus Latin American Reality," Foreign Affairs
(April, 1970), pp. 495-96.

36. As noted earlier, the EEC had established a
special fund, the EDF, in 1957, to provide financial
assistance to the African nations and other countries
associated with the EEC.

37. U.S., Congress, House, National Advisory
Council on International Monetary and Financial Problems, Message from the President of the United States:
Special Report on the Proposed Inter-American Development Bank, 86th Cong., 1st sess., May 11, 1959.

38. For details of the Act of Bogotá, see the
discussion under "Social Development" in Chapter 6,
below.

2

**ORGANIZATION
AND
ADMINISTRATION**

MEMBERSHIP AND VOTING

Only members of the OAS were originally eligible for membership in the IDB. The IDB Charter was signed by twenty Latin American countries and the United States; although Cuba participated in the negotiations for the Charter, it did not actually join the Bank. Trinidad and Tobago joined the IDB in 1967, and Barbados and Jamaica joined in 1969.

As in the case of the World Bank, although the supreme powers of the IDB are vested in a Board of Governors, consisting of one Governor appointed by each member country, the voting power of each Governor is linked to the size of his country's subscription to the Bank. Moreover, authority on all except certain specific matters is delegated to a Board of Executive Directors, in which both representation and voting power are weighted.

Each member country of the IDB has 135 votes, together with one vote for each share of capital stock of the Bank held by that country. The number of votes for each country, as well as the percentage of the total that this represents, is shown in Table 1. Except where otherwise provided in the IDB Agreement, all matters before the Board of Governors are decided by a majority of the total voting power of

TABLE 1

Voting Power in IDB, March 25, 1971

Country of Executive Director and Alternate (A)[a]	Appointed or Elected by	Number of Votes	Percentage of Votes[b]
Argentina	Argentina	34,717	12.42
Peru (A)	Peru	4,769	1.70
		39,486	14.12
Brazil	Brazil	34,717	12.42
Ecuador (A)	Ecuador	1,987	0.71
		36,704	13.13
Honduras	Costa Rica	1,523	0.55
Nicaragua (A)	El Salvador	1,523	0.55
	Guatemala	1,987	0.71
	Haiti	1,523	0.55
	Honduras	1,523	0.55
	Nicaragua	1,523	0.55
		9,602	3.46
Mexico	Barbados	549	0.19
Panama (A)	Dominican Republic	1,987	0.71
	Jamaica	1,987	0.71
	Mexico	22,365	8.00
	Panama	1,523	0.55
		28,411	10.16
Paraguay	Bolivia	2,911	1.04
Bolivia (A)	Paraguay	1,523	0.55
	Uruguay	3,843	1.37
		8,277	2.96
Venezuela	Chile	9,631	3.45
Colombia (A)	Colombia	9,623	3.44
	Trinidad and Tobago	1,523	0.55
	Venezuela	18,663	6.66
		39,440	14.12
United States	United States	117,487	42.05
United States (A)	United States		
Total		279,407	100.00

[a]Symbol (A) indicates countries supplying Alternate Executive Directors.

[b]Details do not add to totals in all cases because of rounding.

Source: IDB, Eleventh Annual Report, 1970 (Washington, D.C., 1971).

38

the member countries.[1] (The voting power of each
Governor corresponds to that shown in Table 1 for
each country.) In such cases, therefore, no individual country has a veto.

The Agreement provides, however, that any increase in the authorized capital stock of the IDB
requires a two-thirds majority of the total number
of Governors representing not less than three-fourths
of the total voting power of the member countries.
A three-fourths majority of the total voting power
is also required for any increase in the resources
of the Fund for Special Operations (FSO), and a similar majority is needed for increasing the number of
Executive Directors, suspending the membership of any
country, terminating the operations of the IDB, and
distributing assets to members in connection with any
winding up of operations. In all these cases, therefore, veto power would lie with the United States,
as well as with various combinations of Latin American members.

Amendments to the Agreement also require a two-
thirds majority of Governors representing three-
fourths of the total voting power of the member countries, except that the unanimous agreement of the
Board of Governors is required for the approval of
any amendment modifying the right to withdraw from
the Bank, to purchase capital stock of the Bank, and
to contribute to the FSO, as well as the limitations
on liability of members laid down in the Agreement.
In certain cases, a two-thirds majority of the total
voting power is required--namely, to authorize the
use of gold or currency held by the Bank for the purchase of other currencies and the investment of funds
not needed in the Bank's operations and to sanction
the operations of the FSO.

The Board of Executive Directors, which functions
continuously in Washington, D.C., conducts the operations of the IDB and exercises all powers other than
those specifically reserved to the Board of Governors.
There were originally seven Executive Directors, one
of whom was appointed by the United States, with the
remaining six being elected by the Governors of the

other member countries under a special procedure.[2]
This special procedure was designed to ensure that
there was fair representation on the Board of Executive Directors for both the smaller and the larger
Latin American countries. (The membership for 1971
is shown in Table 1.) Each Executive Director ap-
points an alternate with full power to act for him
when he is not present; but none of the elected directors and their alternates may be of the same
citizenship.[3]

     In October, 1971, a proposed amendment to the
Agreement was transmitted to the IDB Board of Governors for approval. This amendment would permit the
admission of Canada as a member of the Bank. It
would also permit the admission of "nonregional countries which are members of the International Monetary
Fund and Switzerland. . . . under such general rules
as the Board of Governors shall have established,
subject to such limitations on their rights and obligations, relative to those applicable to regional
members, as the Bank may determine." A related draft
amendment proposed that the number of elected members
of the Board of Executive Directors, which was to be
not less than six (in addition to the member appointed
by the United States), as well as the procedure for
their election, should be determined by the Board of
Governors by a two-thirds majority representing not
less than three-fourths of the total voting power.

     Decisions by the Board of Executive Directors on
the ordinary lending operations of the IDB are subject
to a simple majority rule, so that, here too, no single country has a veto. All decisions concerning the
operations of the FSO, however, require a two-thirds
majority of the total voting power, so that a veto
here would lie with the United States, as well as
with various combinations of Latin American members.
The reason for the difference thus made between the
ordinary and the FSO operations of the Bank is that,
although, at the outset of these operations, the
United States contributed less than one-half of the
subscribed capital of the Bank, it provided two-thirds
of the resources of the FSO.

Although there have been conflicts from time to time on various issues arising within the IDB, it has been possible, in the great majority of cases, to settle them prior to the formal process of voting. On a number of occasions, however, disagreement has persisted and has been reflected in abstentions by various members when the issues in question were put to a vote. There have also been instances where loan proposals have been withdrawn without reaching the stage of being voted upon, since informal consultations between the IDB administration and members of the Board of Executive Directors have indicated that the necessary support would not be forthcoming.

Inevitably, as the chief source of funds, the United States is likely to be in a position to make its views prevail whenever it feels strongly enough on a question to use all the influence at its command. In such cases, the voting procedures of the Bank are a safeguard for the United States, rather than the primary means whereby it secures acceptance of its point of view. Indeed, in a number of cases, the vital importance of enlisting additional resources from the United States has been such as to influence the Latin American members to accept certain changes in policies that could not have been brought about through the exercise of U.S. voting power alone.

This applies, for example, to the decision that loans made with FSO resources out of new contributions during 1971-73 would be repayable in the currencies loaned, rather than in the currencies of the borrowing countries, as had generally been the case previously. (See Chapter 4, below.) If the Latin American countries had sought to exercise their voting power on this matter, they could have prevented this change in policy, but, in that event, of course, the United States would have been free to reconsider the amount of its FSO contribution for 1971-73.

THE PRESIDENT AND HIS STAFF

Following the pattern of the World Bank, the ordinary business of the IDB is conducted by its

President, who is the head of its staff. He is
elected by an absolute majority of Governors representing not less than a majority of the total voting
power. He presides without vote at meetings of the
Board of Executive Directors, except that it is his
duty to cast a deciding vote to break a tie. (The
first President of the IDB was Felipe Herrera of
Chile. He was succeeded, in 1971, by Antonio Ortiz
Mena of Mexico.)

Executive Directors are appointed or elected
for terms of three years and may be reappointed or
re-elected for successive terms. The President of
the IDB, however, holds office for five years and may
also be re-elected to successive terms. The Executive Vice-President is appointed by the Board of
Executive Directors on the recommendation of the
President.

The selection of staff is the responsibility of
the IDB management. Whereas the Executive Directors
represent their governments and receive instructions
accordingly, the President, Executive Vice-President,
other officers, and staff of the IDB owe their duty
entirely to the Bank and recognize no other authority.
Moreover, whereas the membership of the Board of
Executive Directors tends to change from time to
time, as required by the process of appointment and
election, the staff is appointed within the framework
of a career service.

This does not, of course, mean that the membership of the staff does not change; on the contrary,
advantages are seen in having a certain proportion
of staff members returning to their countries after
having acquired experience in the Bank's operations.[4]
But the recruitment of staff follows the procedures
characteristic of the international civil service,
rather than of the selection of government delegates.

Although a high proportion of the senior staff
is provided by the United States, Chile, Argentina,
and Brazil, there is a fairly wide geographic distribution of staff. It is particularly noteworthy
that the United States supplies only one-third of the

top management and a little over one-quarter of the
senior professional staff; this compares with a
share of over 40 per cent in the total authorized
capital of the IDB, as of 1970, and of 75 per cent
in contribution quotas for the FSO.

The staff of the IDB is organized into six departments, each headed by a Manager. In addition to
the Operations Department and the Department of Finance, there are Technical, Legal, and Administrative
Departments, as well as the Secretariat. Attached
to the Office of the President and the Executive
Vice-President are the Program Adviser, the Integration Adviser, and the Auditor-General.

The Managers, Program Adviser, and Integration
Adviser form the membership of the Coordination Committee and of the other top-ranking committees, which,
under the direction of the President or the Executive
Vice-President, make recommendations concerning the
policies or decisions of the IDB. Apart from the
Coordination Committee, other interdepartmental committees include those for loans, technical assistance,
integration, finance, budget, systems analysis, and
salaries and grading.

Following the establishment of CIAP, the IDB
created a high-level programing office, the head of
which--the Program Adviser--ranks among the senior
management officials of the Bank and serves as the
principal staff adviser to the President for the formulation and review of the Bank's development objectives, policies, plans, and programs. The office
maintains close liaison with CIAP and coordinates
IDB policies with those of the Agency for International Development (AID), other U.S. Government agencies, and the World Bank.

THE PROCESSING OF LOANS

There are three stages involved in making a
loan. In the first phase, the Office of the Program
Adviser establishes a loan strategy for each country
based upon the development objectives and priorities

of that country, the studies made by the IDB staff, and the recommendations of CIAP. The strategy includes an indicative estimate of the amounts to be lent over a period of three years and the priority sectors for such lending. Although, in any one year, the IDB may reassign unused funds from one country to another whose project planning is at a more-advanced stage, the Bank's aim over any three-year period is to secure an appropriate balance among loan commitments to each of its member countries. This balance depends upon such factors as population, national income, and debt-servicing capacity.

The drawing up of the strategy and lending program for each country depends not only upon the resources available to the IDB at any particular time but, also, on an assessment of the ability of the country to mobilize the internal resources required in connection with the planned program of borrowing from all the various external sources, as well as to prepare and execute priority projects. The over-all strategy is reviewed by the President and other high officers of the IDB at least twice a year.

Although the adoption of a particular loan strategy provides a framework of reference, rather than a rigid program of lending, it does give the signal for negotiations to begin with the country concerned, for the purpose of drawing up a tentative list of projects to be submitted for IDB financing over the ensuing three-year period. Actual borrowers, whether from the public or the private sector, are then free to submit specific loan requests, which must include a feasibility study and a certification of priority by the government. These requests are considered by the Coordination Committee in the light of recommendations of the various Managers, and the Committee may, if satisfied, then authorize the establishment of a Project Committee.

This leads to the second stage of the lending process, the stage of evaluation. For each project submitted and backed by the requisite information and feasibility study, a team of experts is set up by the IDB under the leadership of the responsible

loan officer. This team is called the Project Committee. Its members usually include a specialist in
the particular sector involved, economists familiar
with the borrowing country and with economic aspects
of the sector, a financial analyst, an institutional
expert where necessary, a member of the Office of
Loan Administration, and a lawyer.

The Project Committee prepares a "loan document"
that provides an over-all evaluation of the project,
including an institutional and administrative evaluation of the borrowing entity. The document includes
annexes devoted to separate technical, economic,
financial, and legal evaluations. The economic evaluation indicates, on the basis of a cost-benefit
analysis or an estimate of the internal rate of return, whether the project is economically sound. The
financial evaluation is designed to establish whether
the borrower will be in a position to service the
debt and to mobilize the complementary financial resources required. In addition, guarantees have to
be provided by the government in the case of government agencies and by national development banks or,
occasionally, commercial banks in the case of private
concerns.

The technical evaluation establishes whether the
project is well conceived in terms of engineering
norms and practice, the availability of inputs, the
scale of output in relation to prospective demand,
the location and design of the plant, and the magni-
tude of investment and probable operating costs. It
also indicates whether the borrowing entity has the
organization and capacity to construct and operate a
plant of the type envisaged. These requirements relate primarily to industrial projects and are, of
course, subject to substantial modification in the
case of projects involving agriculture, infrastructure, housing, or education.

The institutional and administrative evaluation
involves examination of the conditions required to
permit the borrower to carry out the project efficiently and successfully within the economic and social framework of the particular country concerned.

Where weaknesses are revealed, the IDB tries to help by granting technical assistance for the improvement of accounting and cost-control systems, better maintenance of equipment, strengthening management procedures, and so forth. The legal evaluation determines the legal capacity of the borrower to enter into the loan agreement and to fulfill its terms, including the terms of guarantees provided.

In summary, once a project has been properly submitted and has been given the necessary certification of priority by the government concerned, the decision of the IDB on whether to finance it depends primarily on its evaluation of the prospective costs and benefits, although there must also be compliance with certain financial, technical, administrative, and legal requirements deemed indispensable for the success of the project.

After the Project Committee has completed the loan document, it is submitted for approval to the Manager of the Operations Department. From the Operations Manager it goes to the Loan Committee, which consists of all the Managers of departments and Presidential Advisers, meeting under the chairmanship of the Executive Vice-President. After any revision that may be needed, the final loan document is forwarded to the President of the IDB for presentation to the Board of Executive Directors.

The Executive Directors play an active role at this stage, and, in this respect, the procedure differs somewhat from that of other multilateral institutions. In the World Bank, for example, the Executive Directors generally accept the loan as presented by the management. In the IDB, however, the Executive Directors undertake active consultations with the staff and with member governments and conduct an intensive "oral review" of the loan document. At this review, questions are put to the Operations Manager and his staff, as well as to members of the respective Project Committee. The Board of Executive Directors may, on the basis of its review, call for changes to be made in the loan document.

After the Board has approved the loan, a contract is negotiated with the borrower by the Legal Department, acting jointly with the Operations Department. Here again, the procedure contrasts with that of the World Bank, where the loan contract is negotiated in full by the management before Board approval is given.

Once the loan contract has been signed, the Deputy Manager for Loan Administration assumes the responsibility for executing it, with the help of specialists from the office responsible for project analysis and the staff of the field office in the country concerned. At this stage, the Project Committee's work ceases, except in special circumstances where it appears that interdepartmental consultations are required at a high level for introducing modifications into the project.

The third stage of the lending process begins once the loan contract has been signed and a beginning is made in carrying out its terms, prior to the first disbursement. This stage culminates when the entity established by the project begins to function as a going concern and when the IDB begins to evaluate the results. Naturally, the operation is not completed as an IDB activity until all amortization, interest, and commissions falling due have been fully paid.

FIELD OFFICES

In each member country except Barbados and Jamaica, the IDB has an office with a technical staff of project specialists whose number and fields of specialization vary, depending on the size and character of the Bank's portfolio in the particular country concerned. The majority of these project specialists are Latin American technicians--economists, electrical engineers, industrial engineers, and so forth. They all undergo a period of training at IDB headquarters on the Bank's policies and procedures.

Although they are temporary employees, responsible for supervising and inspecting the execution of one or more projects on behalf of the IDB, they may serve the Bank for substantial periods of time if suitable projects are available in one member country or another to which they can be assigned. In this way, the IDB is building up a corps of specialists in project management and execution who can be of service to their own countries, whether in government or private industry. The number of project specialists in the field increased from 38 in 1967 to 115 in 1969; it is expected to rise somewhat further and then to level off.

Clearly, the establishment of field offices by the IDB implies a measure of decentralization of Bank responsibilities. It should be noted that this decentralization is concerned entirely with project execution; it does not apply to the negotiation of loans and the preparation of loan contracts. Although field staffs may provide assistance of various kinds during loan negotiations, broad authority remains vested in headquarters personnel familiar with the Bank's lending policies and programs. Of crucial importance in this context is that each loan must be approved by the Board of Executive Directors in Washington, and the headquarters staff must therefore be thoroughly familiar with each and every project and capable of answering any questions that may be raised.

Even regarding the supervision of project execution, the responsibility of field offices is necessarily limited by the degree of expertise in the various sectors of activity available in each office. Although the existence of field offices makes it possible to reduce the number of headquarters missions, it cannot eliminate them altogether, since the local office may not be competent to form a judgment on the specialized technical aspects of a project. Moreover, it is important for the headquarters staff not to lose touch with the field, especially since the lending activity of the IDB is a continuous process that must always take current developments fully into account.

REVIEW AND AUDIT

The IDB has a system of internal audit, and it
employs Price Waterhouse & Co. as external auditor.[5]
In addition to these conventional forms of auditing,
the IDB decided in March, 1968, to set up a Group of
Controllers to undertake a continuing independent
and comprehensive examination of the manner in which
the Bank is discharging its responsibilities.

The general aim of the Group is to examine
whether the Bank's activities are conducted in a manner designed to attain the objectives intended in an
effective and efficient way and at the lowest reasonable cost. The Group, which consists of three members
selected by the Board of Executive Directors, carries
out its work within the Bank's structure, but independently of management.

The idea of appointing the Group originated with
the Executive Director for the United States. It is
intended that the reports of the Group will be examined by the U.S. National Advisory Council on International Monetary and Financial Policies from the
point of view of the effectiveness of the implementation and administration of loans made by the IDB.
It is also expected that the reports will provide a
basis for suggestions by the U.S. Comptroller-General
to the Secretary of the Treasury and to Congress for
improving the scope of the audit and reporting
standards.[6]

Notwithstanding the existence of these various
checks and controls, the IDB has from time to time
come under criticism regarding the effectiveness of
its operations. There is nothing particularly surprising about this; there is probably not a single
aid institution, whether bilateral or multilateral,
that has escaped such criticism. Development is a
slow and long-term process, and people are understand-
ably impatient to see concrete results.

It has occasionally been alleged that the IDB
administration has tended to be lax and that it has

ventured into types of financing unsuited to a bank.
These criticisms appear to have been based largely
on some of the early lending activities of the IDB,
several of which ran into difficulties. It must be
borne in mind that the IDB was, from the very beginning, required to provide assistance to social projects of a type that had not hitherto received multilateral financing. Indeed, the SPTF was set up by
the United States expressly for this purpose.

There was little to guide the IDB in dealing
with such projects, which raised problems of appraisal
and execution of an entirely different character from
those involved in traditional infrastructure projects,
for which well-recognized evaluation procedures had
existed for some time. Insofar as these problems
were the result of administrative shortcomings, the
IDB was soon able to identify them and to institute
the necessary corrective measures. As a result, the
independent Group of Controllers was able to report,
in 1969, that

> the Inter-American Development Bank is in a
> sound financial position, has successfully
> enlarged its own resources and, on the
> strength of the latter and of the prestige
> it has gained as an international institu-
> tion, has been able to raise additional
> funds by floating bond issues not only in
> the United States but also in Latin Ameri-
> ca, Europe and Asia, and has made flexible
> use of its resources. The Bank's growing
> income has enabled it to improve its admin-
> istration, provide technical assistance to
> member countries, and build up reserves.
> . . . As a general conclusion, it can be
> said that the Bank's financial and adminis-
> trative evolution, as well as its fund-
> raising and lending policies, are sound and
> in keeping with the purposes set forth in
> its charter.[7]

Subsequently, in June and July, 1970, the Committee on Banking and Currency of the U.S. House of

Representatives, as part of its consideration of a
proposal to increase the resources of IDB, conducted
a review of the Bank's operations in the light of
all criticisms known to have been made. In testimony
before the Committee, Secretary of the Treasury David
M. Kennedy expressed the view that "the Bank is a
sound institution operating effectively in support of
the hemisphere's development"; and the Committee,
agreeing with this judgment, concluded that "there
have been no improprieties in the administration of
the Bank," "the Bank is following standard management
procedures," and "the Bank is soundly administered."[8]

Indeed, by 1970, the difficulties experienced
by the IDB in finding enough industrial projects to
finance were being attributed by an independent consulting company, ADELATEC, to the caution and con-
servatism of the Bank's evaluation procedures and its
exacting requirements in making loans.[9] This finding
clearly illustrates the immense difficulty faced by
any development bank in striking exactly the right
balance between careful administration and sound lending policies, on the one hand, and the provision of
prompt and effective support for imaginative schemes
of development, on the other hand.

Since there can be no sustained development without a measure of risk-taking, it would defeat the
basic purposes of the IDB to limit its sphere of activity to projects virtually devoid of uncertainty.
Yet, the Bank's ability to secure funds from capital
markets and even from governments depends to a considerable extent on the degree of confidence that it
generates in the efficiency and viability of its lending activities.

Given the large expansion in resources that the
IDB has been able to mobilize since it was first established,[10] it seems clear that the Bank has succeeded in creating the climate of confidence that is
necessary to this end, albeit at some cost in terms
of its ability to meet the needs of industry and of
certain types of social projects, as will be shown
in Chapter 6, below.

NOTES

1. IDB, Agreement.

2. Ibid., Annex C.

3. Ibid., Art. VIII, sec. 3.

4. T. Graydon Upton, Executive Vice-President
of the IDB, told the National Foreign Trade Convention on November 17, 1970, that "a considerable number of former staff members and former Directors are
now (or recently have been) in such key positions in
our Latin American member countries as Ministers of
Economy, of Finance, of Commerce, or of Justice;
Presidents of Central Banks and public development
banks; Directors of technological institutes and land
reform; Directors and Deputy Directors of Planning
Ministries and Offices; Ambassadors to the White
House; General Managers of Private Banks and Finan-
cieras, Vice Presidents in ADELA and DELTEC, and
last, but not least, the recently elected Mayor of
Quito. Indeed in a recent presidential campaign in
Ecuador, three present or past members of the IDB,
all former cabinet officers, were publicly mentioned
as Presidential candidates."

5. The same company acts as external auditor
for the World Bank.

6. U.S., Congress, House, Committee on Banking
and Currency, Hearing on H.R. 18236, Bill to Amend
the Inter-American Development Bank Act, 91st Cong.,
2d sess., June 30 and July 1, 1970, p. 78. It may
be noted that the Comptroller-General stated his
position on the auditing of activities of international organizations as follows: "We recognize that
U.S. efforts toward improved management of activities
of the international organizations, of which the
United States is a member, must be undertaken and
assessed within the framework of the international
character of the organizations and that membership
presumes a willingness on the part of member nations
to rely on the management of the organization. We

also recognize that constraints on actions that can
be taken unilaterally are an inherent part of such
membership no matter how constructive the proposed
actions might be." Ibid., p. 166.

7. IDB, Group of Controllers of the Review and
Evaluation System, Study of Sources and Uses of
Funds, CRE 1/69-Rev. 2 (Washington, D.C., August,
1969), pp. 1 and 6.

8. U.S., Congress, House, Committee on Banking
and Currency, International Financial Institutions:
Report 91-1300 to Accompany H.R. 18306, 91st Cong.,
2d sess., July 14, 1970, pp. 24-25. Much of the
criticism of inadequate project appraisal evaluated
by the Committee on Banking and Currency had come to
its attention through press accounts of selected
passages from an internal report on the Bank's activities prepared by a consultant, John P. Powelson, at
the Bank's own request. Powelson himself wrote to
Barron's (November 30, 1970, pp. 22-23) pointing out
that the published extracts "did not convey a true
picture of the overall conclusions which I reached
concerning the Bank." He said that his conclusions
were best expressed by the first three paragraphs of
his report, which Barron's had not quoted and which
stated that "the Bank has proved its effectiveness"
and that "the IDB has been more of a true 'development' bank than any similar international institution."

9. For further details, see Chapter 6, below.

10. See Chapter 3, below.

3

The resources of the IDB consist primarily of
its ordinary capital, available for lending on commercial terms, and the FSO, which lends on easy terms.
The IDB also administers funds provided under special
conditions by the United States and various nonmember
countries; these funds are kept entirely separate from
the other operations of the Bank. Decisions taken
at the end of 1970 were designed to increase the
Bank's aggregate resources from a nominal total of
about $6 billion at that time to a level approaching
$10 billion by 1973 (including amounts subscribed in
Latin American currencies). This increase, if implemented, was expected to make possible a rise in
the Bank's total lending volume from just under $650
million a year in 1969-70 to approximately $900 mil-
lion by 1973.

ORDINARY RESOURCES

The Bank's original authorized capital amounted
to $850 million, of which the paid-in portion was
fixed at $400 million, payable in three installments.
The U.S. share of the original paid-in capital was
$150 million, while the share of Latin American mem-
ber countries was $250 million. Payment of these
sums was completed by October, 1962.[1]

That portion of the ordinary capital that did not have to be paid in was the Bank's "callable capital." Following the precedent of the World Bank, the callable capital was not to be used for lending but was to provide a guarantee for IDB borrowings on world capital markets. The initial callable capital was established at $450 million, of which the United States subscribed $200 million and the Latin American countries $231.6 million.[2]

In order to enlarge the Bank's borrowing capacity, the callable capital was increased by approximately $1 billion, to be paid in two installments at the end of 1964 and 1965, respectively, and by a further $1 billion, to be paid in two installments at the end of 1968 and 1970. Thus, the callable portion of the ordinary subscribed capital rose from $431.6 million at the end of 1962 to $2,374.5 million at the end of 1970. The IDB has undertaken, however, not to assume obligations in excess of the callable capital subscribed by the United States; the U.S. share of the Bank's callable capital rose from $200 million at the end of 1962 to $1,023.5 million at the end of 1970.

Against the guarantee provided by the callable subscription of the United States, the IDB had incurred, by the end of 1970, a funded debt totaling $915 million, of which $479 million had been raised in the U.S. market, $361 million in the markets of nonmember countries, and $75 million in Latin America, the latter consisting of issues of two to five years placed with Latin American central banks. As capital markets gained confidence in the IDB and became familiar with its issues, the volume of borrowing that it was able to undertake increased. By the end of 1970, the IDB had virtually exhausted its available ordinary resources, as well as its borrowing capacity, based on unused callable capital.

Since only the callable capital of the IDB was increased during 1964-65 and 1968-70, without any corresponding increase in paid-in capital, the full

impact of the advance in interest rates in world
capital markets was transferred to the Bank's lending
rate, which rose to a level as high as 8.5 per cent
in 1969-70.[3] The Executive Directors of the IDB
therefore concluded in April, 1970, that the only
satisfactory way of keeping the ordinary lending rate
of the Bank within tolerable limits was to provide
for an increase in paid-in capital--the first since
the IDB was founded (except for such minor increases
as resulted from the admission of new members). In
order to reach an annual average volume of ordinary
lending in the range of $300-350 million during the
1971-75 period, the members of the IDB decided to increase the authorized capital stock by $2 billion,
of which $1.6 billion was to be in callable capital
and $400 million in paid-in capital.

One-half of the callable portion was to be subscribed by the middle of 1971, and the remainder by
the middle of 1973. The paid-in capital was to be
subscribed by governments in equal and consecutive
annual installments beginning not later than June 30,
1971, over a three-year period in the case of the
larger countries and over a five-year period for
smaller countries. Table 2 provides details of the
authorized ordinary capital resources of the IDB at
the end of 1970 and the effect of the increase in
resources that was approved at that time.

As in the case of the original subscription,
one-half of the addition to the paid-in capital was
to be in gold or U.S. dollars and one-half in domestic currency. Since the U.S. share was to be $150
million, this meant that the dollar component of the
increase in paid-in capital was to be $268 million.[4]
At the same time, the addition to the Bank's borrowing capacity resulting from the increase in callable
capital subscribed by the United States alone was to
be $673.5 million. To these resources should be
added loan-principal recoveries, which were expected
to rise from an annual rate of $60 million in 1971
to $130 million by 1975, and net income, scheduled
to remain at a level of approximately $20 million.

TABLE 2

Authorized Ordinary Capital Resources
(In Million Dollars)[a]

Country	Paid-In			Callable			Total Capital After Increase	Percentage of Total
	December 31, 1970	1971-75 Increase[b]	Total	December 31, 1970	1971-73 Increase[b]	Total		
Argentina	51.6	51.6	103.1	294.3	191.1	485.4	588.5	12.52
Barbados	2.1	--	2.1	2.1	2.9	5.0	7.0	.15
Bolivia	4.1	4.1	8.3	23.6	15.3	39.0	47.2	1.00
Brazil	51.6	51.6	103.1	294.3	191.1	485.4	588.5	12.52
Chile	14.2	14.2	28.3	80.8	52.5	133.3	161.6	3.44
Colombia	14.2	14.2	28.3	80.7	52.4	133.2	161.5	3.44
Costa Rica	2.1	2.1	4.1	11.8	7.7	19.5	23.6	.50
Dominican Republic	2.8	2.8	5.5	15.8	10.2	26.0	31.5	.67
Ecuador	2.8	2.8	5.5	15.8	10.2	26.0	31.5	.67
El Salvador	2.1	2.1	4.1	11.8	7.7	19.5	23.6	.50
Guatemala	2.8	2.8	5.5	15.8	10.2	26.0	31.5	.67
Haiti	2.1	2.1	4.1	11.8	7.7	19.5	23.6	.50
Honduras	2.1	2.1	4.1	11.8	7.7	19.5	23.6	.50
Jamaica	2.8	2.8	5.5	15.8	10.2	26.0	31.5	.67
Mexico	33.2	33.2	66.3	189.2	122.9	312.0	378.3	8.05
Nicaragua	2.1	2.1	4.1	11.8	7.7	19.5	23.6	.50
Panama	2.1	2.1	4.1	11.8	7.7	19.5	23.6	.50
Paraguay	2.1	2.1	4.1	11.8	7.7	19.5	23.6	.50
Peru	6.9	6.9	13.8	39.4	25.6	65.0	78.9	1.68
Trinidad and Tobago	2.1	2.1	4.1	11.8	7.7	19.5	23.6	.50
United States	150.0	150.0	300.0	1,023.5	673.5	1,697.0	1,997.0	42.47
Uruguay	5.5	5.5	11.1	31.6	20.5	52.0	63.1	1.34
Venezuela	27.6	27.6	55.3	157.7	102.4	260.0	315.3	6.71
Subtotal	388.5	386.4	774.9	2,374.5	1,552.6	3,927.1	4,702.0	100.00
Unassigned[c]	86.5	13.6	100.1	300.5	47.5	347.9	448.0	
Total	475.0	400.0	875.0	2,675.0	1,600.0	4,275.0	5,150.0	

[a]Details do not add to totals in all cases because of rounding.
[b]Approved on December 31, 1970.
[c]Amounts unassigned and reserved for new members.

Source: IDB, Proposal for an Increase in the Resources of the Inter-American Development Bank (Washington, D.C., April, 1970).

58

FUND FOR SPECIAL OPERATIONS

The FSO constitutes a soft-loan facility of the IDB. In the past, its terms have included repayment in local currency, as well as longer maturities and lower interest rates than those for ordinary loans.[5] The FSO derives its resources from special subscriptions by member governments.

The initial resources of the FSO amounted to $146.3 million, of which $100 million were supplied by the United States, the remainder being contributed by the Latin American countries, one-half in U.S. dollars and one-half in their national currencies. In January, 1964, contributions were increased by the equivalent of $73.2 million, of which the United States provided $50 million.

In March, 1965, a relatively large increase of $900 million in FSO resources was approved, reflecting the decision to discontinue the loan operations of the SPTF, discussed below, and merge them with the FSO. The U.S. share of the increase was $750 million, while the Latin American members contributed $150 million in their national currencies, payment being made in three installments between the middle of 1965 and the end of 1966. In 1967, a further $1.2 billion expansion of FSO resources was approved, also payable in three equal installments by the end of 1969. The U.S. share on this occasion was $900 million, the remainder being contributed in the national currencies of the Latin American countries.

The balance of FSO resources available at the end of 1970 amounted to some $300 million, while loan activity was in excess of $400 million a year. Thus, resources were not expected to be sufficient to cover 1971 loan activity, and it was decided to increase FSO resources by the equivalent of $1,500 million, payable in three installments from 1971 to 1973. Of this increase, $1 billion was to be contributed by the United States and $500 million by the Latin American countries in their own currencies. Table 3 shows the cumulative total of resources contributed

to the FSO by the end of 1970 and the effect of the
approved increase for 1971-73.

The Latin American countries have gradually been
increasing their share of new resources allocated to
the FSO from one-fifth of the total expansion in 1965
to one-third of the increase for 1971-73. This advance must, however, be interpreted in the light of
the fact that since 1964 all Latin American contributions to FSO resources have been made in national
currencies; and these currencies have been used
mainly in conjunction with FSO loans to the countries
that contributed them.

As an explicit recognition of the importance of
mutual cooperation among the Latin American countries,
however, the four Latin American members with the
largest FSO contribution quotas--Argentina, Brazil,
Mexico, and Venezuela--agreed, in connection with
the 1967 replenishment, that a portion of their new
contributions should be made available to cover local
costs in other countries, in addition to financing
exports under IDB projects. Subsequently, Chile and
Colombia were added to this group, in connection
with the 1971-73 replenishment.

SOCIAL PROGRESS TRUST FUND

The SPTF was created under an agreement between
the United States and the IDB in June, 1961. There
had been a growing demand for programs of social development, and, in September, 1960, the OAS Committee
of Twenty-one, meeting in Bogotá, proposed that part
of the $500 million that the U.S. Congress had au-
thorized for Latin American aid should be used to
finance a special inter-American fund for social development, to be administered primarily by the IDB.

Following the appropriation of this sum in May,
1961, President Kennedy allocated $394 million for
SPTF, in line with the OAS request. An important
feature of the new program was the acceptance by the
Latin American countries of an obligation to take
adequate measures of self-help, notably regarding

TABLE 3

Resources of FSO
(In Million Dollars)[a]

Country	Contributions, as of December 31, 1970	1971-73 Increase[b]	Contributions After Increase
Argentina	115.1	109.0	224.1
Barbados	.4	.4	.8
Bolivia	9.2	8.8	18.0
Brazil	115.1	109.0	224.1
Chile	31.6	29.9	61.5
Colombia	31.6	29.9	61.5
Costa Rica	4.6	4.4	9.0
Dominican Republic	6.2	5.8	12.0
Ecuador	6.2	5.8	12.0
El Salvador	4.6	4.4	9.0
Guatemala	6.2	5.8	12.0
Haiti	4.6	4.4	9.0
Honduras	4.6	4.4	9.0
Jamaica	6.2	5.8	12.0
Mexico	74.0	70.1	144.1
Nicaragua	4.6	4.4	9.0
Panama	4.6	4.4	9.0
Paraguay	4.6	4.4	9.0
Peru	15.4	14.6	30.0
Trinidad and Tobago	4.6	4.4	9.0
United States	1,800.0	1,000.0	2,800.0
Uruguay	12.3	11.7	24.0
Venezuela	61.7	58.4	120.1
Total	2,328.0	1,500.0	3,828.0

[a]Details do not add to totals in all cases because of rounding.
[b]Approved on December 31, 1970.

Source: IDB, Proposal for an Increase in the Resources of the Inter-American Development Bank (Washington, D.C., April, 1970).

61

taxation, the ownership and use of land, and the improvement of education and training, health facilities, and housing conditions.

The agreement authorized the IDB to make loans
in the fields of land settlement and improved land
use, housing for low-income groups, community water
supply and sanitation facilities, and supplementary
financing of facilities for advanced education and
training related to economic and social development.
In addition, it was authorized to provide technical
assistance related to those fields and to the mobilization of domestic financial resources. The IDB accepted the administration of the SPTF for these purposes. In February, 1964, the United States raised
the amount of the SPTF to $525 million.

It was decided, in 1965, that no new resources
should be sought for the SPTF, but that, in the future, FSO operations should include social development programs, including those previously financed
through the SPTF. One factor underlying this decision was that, although the resources of the SPTF
were supplied entirely by the United States, the
Latin American countries were contributing to the
FSO, so that the shift to the FSO was in line with
ideas of promoting self-help by the borrowing countries. An additional consideration may have been
some uncertainty about the success of the social
projects undertaken within the SPTF program and a
desire to reduce the degree of concessionality and
flexibility attached to such projects, notably regarding the financing of local costs in foreign
exchange.

No loans have been made from the SPTF since
1965, but remaining resources have been employed for
technical-assistance activities. Available resources,
including repayments, have been utilized to purchase
participations in FSO loans that were financing SPTF-
type projects; by the end of 1969, total SPTF purchases of such participations amounted to $66.4
million.

RESOURCES FROM NONMEMBER
COUNTRIES

The IDB has entered into agreements with Canada,
the Federal Republic of Germany, Norway, Sweden, the
United Kingdom, and the Vatican to administer special
funds that they have provided for development projects in Latin America, to be financed on concessional
terms. In addition, the IDB also administers a loan
for $1.3 million that the Intergovernmental Committee
for European Migration made for agricultural projects
in Brazil.

At the end of December, 1970, these various arrangements totaled $85 million, of which the largest
single amount was the Canadian Fund, amounting to
60 million Canadian dollars. In effect, the IDB is
responsible for channeling $10 million of Canadian
assistance to Latin America every year. In addition,
the IDB has entered into arrangements with Canada
and the Netherlands under which it is responsible
for channeling into Latin American development a total
of $50 million, provided by these two countries
through parallel or independent financing arrangements.

The IDB has also placed a large number of long-
term bond issues in nonmember countries and has entered into a variety of parallel financing arrangements and sales of participations. As noted earlier,
IDB borrowings in eleven nonmember countries reached
the equivalent of $361 million at the end of 1970,
out of a total funded debt of $915 million. It may
be observed that nearly $250 million of the borrowing
from nonmembers was raised during 1968-70 alone.

In October, 1967, the IDB had adopted a policy
designed to exert strong pressure on nonmember countries to make resources available to the IDB. This
decision followed a study carried out in June and
July, 1967, as a result of which the Executive Directors concluded that "the possibility of obtaining
substantial additional funds from developed countries

in the foreseeable future is relatively small under existing circumstances." The Executive Directors therefore decided that, from the beginning of 1968,

> a country in a reasonably advanced stage of development will be considered eligible for procurement under loans from the ordinary capital resources of the Bank and the unrestricted resources of the Bank's Fund for Special Operations in any given period only if, up to a date shortly before the beginning of the period, the country has provided resources to the Bank on reasonable terms in a cumulative amount bearing an acceptable percentage relationship to cumulative procurement already effected in such country. The ratio of financing to procurement will be 100 per cent.[6]

This policy appears to have been effective in persuading European countries and Japan to take up a larger quantity of IDB bonds than they might otherwise have done, although the consequential restriction on IDB procurement might have had the effect of increasing project costs in cases where the prices of the cheapest eligible suppliers were above world market levels. Direct loans have been obtained from a number of nonmember countries. The IDB also raises funds by transfers or sales from its ordinary loan portfolio to various financial institutions in nonmember countries, as well as in the United States, and also to certain international financial organizations.

As noted in Chapter 2, above, the Board of Governors has received a proposal whereby membership in the IDB would be open to Canada and certain other developed countries. The hoped-for advantage is that additional ordinary capital resources, including paid-in capital, would be subscribed and that access to capital markets by the IDB would be made easier. Membership might also elicit a substantially greater volume of concessional funds than countries would be prepared to make available as nonmembers.

One question that arises is whether an enlargement of membership along these lines would affect
the regional character of the IDB. The view of the
U.S. Government is that it would not. Latin American
views have been less clear-cut. Although advantages
have been seen in diversifying the sources of funds
for the IDB, concern has been expressed about any
basic change in the inter-American character of the
Bank. Moreover, many of the Latin American countries
would be particularly reluctant to lose their majority
vote in the IDB.

On the other hand, some Latin American countries
have become concerned at the increasing U.S. scrutiny
of IDB operations along the lines described later in
this chapter. Under such conditions, as they see it,
a formal superiority of voting power in the hands of
the Latin American members may count for little, especially since the United States has a decisive voice
in determining the amount and distribution of FSO
funds. For these reasons, some countries see advantages in a diversification of IDB membership among
developed countries, so that any one donor country is
less likely to be able to rule the roost.[7]

Doubts have been expressed about whether developed countries outside the western hemisphere would
substantially enlarge their aid to Latin American
countries even if they were offered full membership
in the IDB. Although a number of European countries
and Japan are expecting to increase the over-all
volume of their assistance, they seem likely to give
priority to the needs of poorer countries in Africa
and Asia.

THE SUPPLY OF FUNDS:
PROBLEMS AND ISSUES

The total funds effectively available to the IDB
from various sources at the end of 1969 are listed
in Table 4. The resources are divided into three
main types: those that had been lent or subscribed
by governments and central banks; receipts in respect

of interest and other charges on past lending; and
funds received from sales of bonds, other securities,
or participations to private financial institutions
or investors.

Funds raised from private investors accounted
for less than one-sixth of the total resources supplied to the IDB by the end of 1969, whereas governmental and central bank subscriptions, together with
interest on the Bank's loans to its members, furnished more than five-sixths of the total. Even if
amounts in Latin American currencies are excluded,
the funds supplied from public sources were four
times as large as were those from private sources.
The question that arises is whether the difficulties
involved in the use of funds borrowed from private
sources are justified by the relatively small volume
of resources thereby made available.

One major advantage of funds borrowed from the
private sector is that their use is not directly
subject to the veto of any one country. Moreover,
they are not subject to being tied to the exports of
a donor country as are subscriptions to the FSO. On
the other hand, as will be shown in Chapter 4, below,
the mounting cost of bond flotations has made it
necessary to raise interest charges on ordinary IDB
lending from 5.75 per cent in 1962 to 8.2 per cent
in 1969-70, for reasons that took no account of the
development needs or balance-of-payments position of
the borrowing countries. World Bank experience was
similar, although, for reasons discussed in Chapter
4, below, it was possible to hold down the increase
in interest charges to some extent.

Government contributions to the soft-lending
facilities of the IDB and the World Bank Group have
been of considerable help, but they have by no means
sufficed to generate an adequate supply of multilateral lending facilities on terms appropriate to the
debt-servicing capacity of the majority of the member
countries of these institutions. The result is that
there is severe competition among the developing
countries for the very limited funds available on
easy terms.

TABLE 4

Composition of IDB Resources, December 31, 1969
(In Million Dollars)

Resource	In All Currencies	In Convertible Currencies
From Public Sources		
Government subscriptions		
Paid-in capital	388.5	269.2
FSO	2,328.0	1,835.0
SPTF	485.0	485.0
Funds in administration	69.8	69.8
Subtotal	3,271.3	2,659.0
Public loans and bond purchases	99.4	99.4
Total public sources	3,370.7	2,758.4
From Service on IDB Loans		
Interest, commitment charges, and commissions	214.3	145.1
From Private Sources		
Sales of bonds and private loans	667.8	667.8
Sales of participations in loans, less repayments	25.0	25.0
Total private sources	692.8	692.8
Grand total	4,277.8	3,596.3

Source: IDB.

In the case of IDA, for example, out of approximately $3.3 billion committed up to the middle of
1971, 60 per cent went to India and Pakistan and most
of the remainder to a number of African countries,
leaving only $177 million available for twelve Latin
American countries. There were, of course, important
reasons for this apparently one-sided distribution.
Since IDA's resources were inadequate, they had to
be rationed on the basis of some set of objective
criteria, including the level of per capita income.

India and Pakistan are not only among the poorest countries in the world but, also, among the
largest in terms of population, accounting for more
than 56 per cent of the population of developing
countries eligible for IDA credits. Similarly, the
very low levels of income and development in the African countries clearly give them priority over many
of the Latin American countries with respect to access to IDA lending facilities. Moreover, the availability of FSO loans on easy terms to Latin American
countries is a factor to be taken into account in
determining the distribution of IDA resources. All
this does not mean, however, that the total volume
of resources available for lending to Latin American
countries on soft terms is sufficient in the light
of their borrowing requirements and debt-servicing
capacity.

THE BRETTON WOODS CONCEPT
OF MULTILATERAL LENDING

Thus, the basic conception of the World Bank and
of the IDB as institutions concerned with channeling
resources from private capital markets to the developing countries has come increasingly into conflict
with the need to provide resources to these countries
on terms corresponding to their debt-servicing capacities. And, while a serious effort has been made to
correct the imbalance by setting up soft-loan facilities with the aid of direct government contributions,
the remedy provided remains inadequate for the scope
of the task.

There is, however, an even more fundamental
sense in which the Bretton Woods conception of multilateral lending, as applied to the World Bank and
the IDB, requires reconsideration. Under the Bretton
Woods concept, the multilateral lending institutions
must be guided in their policies not merely by the
views and attitudes of their member governments, particularly of the capital-exporting countries, but,
also, by the need to maintain the highest possible
standing in the world's capital markets.

Both institutions pride themselves on their
bonds having been given the triple-A rating in the
U.S. capital market.[8] The criteria applied by Standard and Poor, however, in determining the credit
rating of the World Bank and the IDB are not necessarily the same as those that would be considered
most relevant and most appropriate from the standpoint of promoting development in the developing
countries.

The need to maintain the highest credit standing
has frequently been cited as a decisive consideration militating against policy changes regarded as
desirable from the point of view of development. As
noted earlier, the idea of combining soft-lending
facilities with more conventional loans on commercial
terms within the same institution[9] was resisted for
many years, in part because of the fear that this
would undermine market confidence in the lending
practices and policies of the World Bank.

This fear proved groundless in the end, since
IDA was established within the World Bank Group without adverse effects on the Bank's creditworthiness.
Similar fears have been expressed regarding the proposal to provide subsidies on multilateral lending
and to furnish general balance-of-payments support
for soundly conceived development programs in addition
to loans for specific projects.

A recent example of inhibitions on policy caused
by fear of capital-market reaction is to be found in
the report of a group of experts appointed by the IDB

to analyze the possibility of establishing a regional
finance corporation for Latin American industry.[10]
The experts agreed that a special institution should
be established for this purpose and that a "clear relation" should exist between this institution and the
IDB, accompanied by substantial financial support
from the latter to the former.

The obvious way of doing this would be to amend
the IDB Agreement to authorize the Bank to participate
in subscriptions to capital stock. The experts concluded, however, that "even if the Agreement [setting
up the IDB] were to be amended in this respect, it
is possible that investment by the IDB in the stock
of the new institution would have a negative effect
on its access to bond markets in industrialized
countries."[11]

In view of this, it was agreed that the IDB
should be limited to making long-term loans to the
new institution and contributing resources to a fund
for the promotion of projects "which would enable
the corporation to perform its tasks without incurring loss during its first years of operation." It
therefore appears that a considerable price in terms
of policy rigidity and the need to resort to cumbersome circumlocutions has to be paid for the resources
secured from capital markets.

It is difficult to determine how far private investors are, or might be, deterred by policy changes
of the type referred to above. It is arguable that
the danger of default by any borrower from the IDB
as a result of what bondholders might regard as
questionable lending policies, defective project appraisal, or any other shortcoming would, in practice,
be a matter of little consequence for the investor,
since the security of the bonds is insured through
the backing of the uncalled capital available from
the U.S. Government. Whether or not this is a correct appraisal of investor psychology, the fear of
capital-market reaction certainly appears to have
influenced decisions on lending policies from time
to time, and, yet, it hardly seems likely that investors in bonds are the people best placed to decide
such matters.

Thus, whether one looks at the matter from the point of view of the factors governing lending policies or from the standpoint of the terms on which assistance should be provided to developing countries, it would seem desirable to reconsider the manner in which resources are made available to the multilateral lending institutions, including the IDB. While the Bretton Woods concept of channeling resources from private capital markets to developing countries could, perhaps, be retained as a useful auxiliary device, there is a strong case for concluding that the principal emphasis should henceforth be placed upon government subscriptions.

Some would see a disadvantage in such a tendency, in that, although the multilateral institutions would thereby become less dependent on private capital markets, they would become correspondingly more dependent on governments. Undue government interference might cause serious difficulties for the multilateral agencies. An indication of the type of problem involved was given by Congressional action on the proposal for U.S. contributions to the ordinary capital of the IDB and to the FSO during the years 1971-73, as described below.

On December 30, 1970, Congress specifically authorized the U.S. Governor of the IDB to enter into a multilateral commitment to replenish the resources of the Bank--that is, "to vote in favor of the two resolutions proposed by the Governors at their annual meeting in April 1970," which provided for the contributions indicated in Tables 2 and 3.[12] But it undermined the significance of its own action by two related decisions.

The first of these decisions resulted from strong Congressional criticism of the whole concept of soft loans through the FSO--a concept that is a fundamental element in the Agreement establishing the IDB.[13] The prevailing view was that Congress should make a study of past experience with such loans before agreeing to authorize the second and third installments of the U.S. contribution to the FSO, amounting to $450 million in each of the years 1972 and 1973.

Thus, although, at the end of 1970, Congress in principle confirmed the U.S. Government's commitment to the new contributions for 1971-73, it provided so far as the FSO was concerned, only for the first-year authorization of $100 million and made the second and third installments contingent upon authorizations and appropriations to be considered later. This represented a new departure in the Congressional method of voting funds for the FSO, since previous practice would have been to authorize the entire $1 billion from the beginning. There would still have been a need to make the requisite appropriations, but these had, in the past, invariably provided the amounts authorized. The new procedure was bound to create serious uncertainty regarding the basis on which future FSO operations should be planned.

The new approach was coupled with provision for the U.S. National Advisory Council on International Monetary and Financial Policies to submit annual reports on each loan made by the IDB, as well as by the World Bank, IDA, and the Asian Development Bank (ADB). These reports were to evaluate every new loan and were to indicate "how each loan will benefit the people of the recipient country." In addition, in the case of the IDB only, reports were to be made on the "steps taken jointly and individually by member countries of the Inter-American Development Bank to restrain their military expenditures, and to preserve and strengthen free and democratic institutions."[14] Moreover, the House of Representatives made known its view that "on approved loans the report should indicate whether the United States representative voted for or against the loan."[15] If this approach were generalized and legislatures all over the world began to examine the details of every loan made by the multilateral agencies, the usefulness of these agencies would come into serious question.

The second decision, which also involved a critical departure from past practice, took place when the time came for the subscription to the ordinary capital of the IDB to be appropriated in 1971. Despite the clear commitment implied in the decision of December 30, 1970, Congress subsequently failed to

appropriate the amounts that it had itself authorized.
Thus, Congress appropriated only $200 million of the
$336.8 million due by way of subscription to the
callable capital and only $25 million of the $50 million due for the first installment of the paid-in
capital subscription. Consequently, the entire increase in the ordinary resources of the IDB had to be
postponed.

Apart from the effects of this action on the
current operations of the IDB, it raised the most
serious questions about the future ability of the
U.S. Government to enter into international negotiations concerning financial commitments not only to
the IDB but, also, to all the other multilateral financial agencies. As pointed out by the Under-Secretary of the Treasury at the time,

> once we have agreed, pursuant to Congres-
> sional authority, to accept and perform
> under an international understanding for
> financing an institution, it is a breach
> of an international commitment to fail to
> meet our subsequent annual financial obli-
> gations. Such a breach damages our ability
> to negotiate convincingly and advantageously
> in the future.[16]

It might be thought that the danger of external
interference in the lending policies of the multilateral agencies would be lessened to the extent that
their sources of finance were diversified and that
this would suggest a need to maintain a large flow
of funds from private capital markets, as well as
from governments. Although there is something in
this, its significance cannot be pressed very far.
In the first place, private capital markets can provide the resources only for hard lending and not for
concessional lending.

Second, governments can withhold permission for
the sale of bonds in their capital markets just as
readily as they can reduce their own direct subscriptions, in the event that they feel they have cause
for complaint against one of the multilateral agencies.

Third, the above-mentioned failure of Congress to replenish the callable capital of the IDB in the pre-agreed amounts required, at a time when the Bank had reached the limit of its borrowing capacity against the existing callable capital, clearly indicated that the United States would, in effect, be able, if it so chose, to acquire almost the same degree of control over the ordinary operations of the IDB that it already had over the FSO. Thus, the independence resulting from the right to sell IDB obligations in private capital markets may be more apparent than real.[17]

Excessive surveillance by governments and by investors in bonds could curtail the freedom of action of the multilateral financial institutions to an extent that would seriously prejudice their ability to respond adequately to the development needs of member countries. Clearly, it would be undesirable for the staffs of the multilateral agencies to operate in a political vacuum, without regard to the views of those on whom they depend for their resources. At the same time, the system of multilateral assistance could not work effectively if the power of the governmental purse were to be used to impose excessive checks and balances and if these were combined with restraints on prudent risk-taking induced by fears of capital-market reaction.

NOTES

1. Since Cuba did not join the IDB, the total amount actually paid in by October, 1962, was $381.6 million, rather than the $400 million originally envisaged. Paid-in capital was subscribed half in gold or U.S. dollars and half in member currencies or nonnegotiable noninterest-bearing demand notes. Consequently, $265.8 million out of the $381.6 million of paid-in capital was in U.S. dollars, the remainder consisting of Latin American currencies.

2. Here, again, the shortfall was due to the fact that Cuba did not join.

3.   The lending rate of the World Bank did not
go above 7.25 per cent during this period.   The difference between the lending rates of the World Bank
and the IDB occurred because the latter rate reflected
not only the higher average cost of borrowed funds
to the more recently established IDB, but, also, a
margin of 1.25 per cent, consisting of 1 per cent to
cover the commission required by the IDB Charter and
.25 per cent to help meet administrative costs.   The
World Bank abolished its commission charge in 1964,
when its reserves reached $950 million.   The World
Bank's lending rate was actually lower than was its
average borrowing rate during 1969-70.

4.   At the end of 1970, paid-in capital subscribed by the Latin American countries totaled
$238.5 million, of which $119.2 million was in dollars.   The increase approved on December 31, 1970,
amounted to $236.4 million, of which $118.2 million
was in dollars.

5.   As noted in Chapter 4, below, the terms and
conditions of FSO lending were changed in connection
with the 1970 replenishment of FSO resources.

6.   IDB press release, October 15, 1967.   The
list of countries to which the new policy was to apply was as follows: Australia, Austria, Belgium,
Canada, Denmark, Finland, France, the Federal Republic
of Germany, Italy, Japan, Kuwait, Luxembourg, the
Netherlands, New Zealand, Norway, the Union of South
Africa, Sweden, Switzerland, and the United Kingdom.
These were the so-called Part I countries of IDA,
together with Switzerland.

7.   See also the statement of the President of
the IDB regarding complaints made by Peru and other
members, referred to in Chapter 7, below.

8.   The World Bank points out (100 Questions and
Answers [Washington, D.C., March, 1970], p. 66) that,
in 1947, its bonds only qualified for an A rating--
the third highest--but that, since 1959, they have
been accorded the triple-A rating.

9. Although a single administration runs the
World Bank and IDA and there is no difference between
the types of projects financed, other than the terms
on which resources are provided, the two agencies are
formally regarded as separate entities, drawing their
funds from different sources--the World Bank from
paid-in capital and borrowing from capital markets
and IDA from government contributions.

10. IDB, Analysis of the Possible Formation of
a Regional Finance Corporation for the Expansion of
Latin American Industry (Washington, D.C., August,
1970). [Hereafter referred to as Analysis.]

11. Ibid., p. 2.

12. U.S. Code, Congressional and Administrative
News, 91st Cong., 2d sess., 1970, I, Laws (Public
Law 91-599; 84 Stat. 1657 [H.R. 18306], ch. 2, 1932.

13. The question of the terms of IDB lending is
considered in Chapter 4, below.

14. Ibid., ch. 3.

15. See U.S., Congress, House, 91st Cong., 2d
sess., Congressional Record, CXVI, 206, December 21,
1970, H 12239.

16. Statement of Charles E. Walker, Under-Secretary of the Treasury, before the Subcommittee on Foreign Operations of the Senate Appropriations Committee,
on fiscal year 1972 appropriations for international
financial institutions, June 8, 1971.

17. As indicated in Chapter 7, below, the President of the IDB considers the best safeguard to be
the admittance of other developed countries to membership in the IDB in the hope of creating competition
among the capital-exporting countries, thereby improving the chances for a liberalization of conditions
and policies.

POLICIES AFFECTING
ORDINARY LOANS

From the initiation of its activities up to the
end of 1970, the IDB made loans out of its ordinary
resources in an amount exceeding $1,486 million.
Projects were financed in all member countries except
Barbados, Jamaica, and Trinidad and Tobago, which had
only recently become members, and Bolivia and Haiti,
which received loans only from the FSO. Loans from
the ordinary resources of the IDB were allocated to
all sectors financed by the Bank except education
and housing.

Because the ordinary resources of the IDB consist mainly of funds borrowed in capital markets,
where the cost of capital has been rising, the Bank
has been obliged to increase its interest charges
continuously. When the IDB began its operations,
the basic interest rate for ordinary loans was fixed
at 5.75 per cent. This basic rate was increased by
stages and reached a level of 8 per cent in April,
1969,[1] which was maintained during the remainder of
1969 and throughout 1970.

The interest charge payable by the borrower
covers not only the cost of the borrowed funds but,
also, a commission of 1 per cent, as provided in the

IDB Charter, and a charge of .25 per cent to help
meet administrative costs. A special service commission of .5 per cent is added to the 8 per cent interest rate whenever the cost of resources borrowed by
the IDB exceeds 6.75 per cent.[2]

The IDB levies a commitment charge on unused
balances of loans, affecting both the foreign-exchange
and local currency components. This charge covers
the spread between the interest rate at which the
IDB borrows and the short-term yield that it obtains
on the borrowed funds pending their disbursement
against particular projects. In other words, it represents the cost to the IDB of holding money available for disbursement. The charge, which begins to
accrue sixty days after the date of the signing of
the contract, amounts to 1.25 per cent, at an annual
rate, in the case of loans where the cost to the IDB
is not in excess of 6.75 per cent, and 2 per cent,
at an annual rate, on money borrowed at rates higher
than 6.75 per cent.

Payments for amortization, interest, and service
commissions must be made in the currencies borrowed,
whereas the commitment charge is payable in the currency committed. In the case of local currency loans,
payment must be made in an amount determined by the
dollar equivalent, at the 1959 gold parity. Although,
in general, the obligation to maintain the value of
payments in terms of dollars rests upon the borrower,
in certain countries the respective governments have
assumed this responsibility.

The IDB applies flexible criteria regarding the
period of amortization and takes into account the
character of the project, the borrower's capacity to
pay, and the debt-servicing capacity of the country
concerned. Loans authorized in 1970 were extended
for terms ranging from twelve to twenty years.[3]

In fixing grace periods (that is, the length of
time that elapses before the first amortization payments fall due), the main consideration, in principle,
is the time required for the project to begin to
yield returns. In practice, the grace period is

usually fixed at six months in excess of the time
estimated for completion of the project. In general,
the IDB tries to avoid grace periods in excess of
three and one-half years in the case of projects financed from the ordinary capital of the Bank.

Table 5 sets forth the distribution of interest
rates on IDB loans outstanding at the end of 1969.
Tables 6-8 provide comparative data on interest rates,
maturities, and grace periods for four of the major
lending agencies; for the IDB, these latter tables
represent a weighted average of all operations of the
Bank, whether from ordinary, FSO, or SPTF resources.

As can be seen from these tables, an effort has
been made by the IDB to adjust the terms of lending
to the degree of development of the recipient countries. The least developed countries borrowed, in
1969, at the lowest interest rates and with the
longest average maturities and grace periods.[4]

The total charge levied by the IDB on its ordinary loans has been higher than that applicable to
the loans of the World Bank for two main reasons.
First, the World Bank has had resources at its dis-
posal that have been accumulating over a period of
more than twenty years; the average historical cost
of these resources was therefore lower than was the
cost of funds available to the more recently established IDB. Second, the IDB is required to charge a
1 per cent commission to build up its Special Reserve,
whereas the World Bank already has very large reserves
and, therefore, has been able to dispense with such
a commission since 1964.

POLICIES AFFECTING FSO LOANS

Up until the end of 1970, the IDB had made loans
from the FSO totaling more than $2,021 million. All
member countries had received such loans except Barbados, which had joined the IDB relatively recently.
FSO loans, which carry easier terms than do ordinary
loans, are designed for "special circumstances" affecting particular countries or projects that make

TABLE 5

Distribution of IDB Loans in Terms of Interest Rates
Charged, 1961-69
(In Million U.S.-Dollar Equivalents)

Source	Interest Rates Charged				
	3 Per Cent or Less	3.01-5 Per Cent	5.01-6 Per Cent	6.01 Per Cent and Over	Total
Ordinary capital	--	3.7	685.4	605.0	1,294.1
FSO	607.6	970.7	3.3	--	1,581.6
SPTF	496.2	--	--	--	496.2
Other	56.1	--	--	1.7	57.8
Total	1,159.9	974.4	688.7	606.7	3,429.7

Source: IDB.

it inadvisable to use the ordinary resources of the
IDB.[5] Among the countries that received two-thirds
or more of their loans from the IDB through the FSO
or the SPTF between 1961 and 1969 were Bolivia, the
Dominican Republic, Ecuador, Haiti, Paraguay, Peru,
Trinidad and Tobago, and the Central American
countries.

Until 1971, FSO loans carried two different interest rates: 3 per cent on predominantly social
projects and 4 per cent on economic projects. In
both cases, a service commission of .75 per cent was
included. The commission was payable proportionately
in the currency disbursed, whereas the remaining
2.25 per cent and 3.25 per cent, respectively, were
repayable in the same currency as the principal.[6]

TABLE 6

Average Interest Rates on Loans Authorized, 1961 and 1969
(In Per Cent)

Country Groups	AID		EXIMBANK		IBRD[a]		IDB[b]	
	1961	1969	1961	1969	1961	1969	1961	1969
Advanced[c]	0.77	2.38	5.75	6.00	5.75	6.70	5.42	5.46
Medium[d]	1.97	3.04	5.75	6.00	4.38	6.58	3.14	4.24
Less Developed[e]	3.21	2.84	5.75	6.00	4.07	5.92	3.98	3.17
All	1.87	2.81	5.75	6.00	4.57	6.46	3.92	4.66

[a]IBRD includes IDA.
[b]IDB includes FSO.
[c]Argentina, Brazil, and Mexico.
[d]Chile, Colombia, Peru, Uruguay, and Venezuela.
[e]All other countries of Latin America.

Source: IDB.

TABLE 7

Average Maturities on Loans Authorized, 1961 and 1969
(In Years)

Country Groups	AID		EXIMBANK		IBRD[a]		IDB[b]	
	1961	1969	1961	1969	1961	1969	1961	1969
Advanced[c]	29.81	30.00	9.68	6.13	13.59	16.40	11.54	17.08
Medium[d]	19.17	30.00	6.01	6.40	21.20	14.15	18.24	18.55
Less Developed[e]	18.36	28.20	8.34	10.60	23.50	19.26	14.59	19.41
All	21.83	29.34	7.12	6.89	20.33	16.46	15.68	17.94

[a]IBRD includes IDA.
[b]IDB includes FSO.
[c]Argentina, Brazil, and Mexico.
[d]Chile, Colombia, Uruguay, and Venezuela.
[e]All other countries of Latin America.

Source: IDB.

TABLE 8

Average Grace Periods on Loans Authorized, 1961 and 1969
(In Years)

Country Groups	AID		EXIMBANK		IBRD[a]		IDB[b]	
	1961	1969	1961	1969	1961	1969	1961	1969
Advanced[c]	10.01	10.00	2.02	4.02	3.68	4.43	3.74	4.02
Medium[d]	7.04	9.55	2.17	2.69	6.07	4.09	1.90	4.10
Less Developed[e]	2.84	8.69	3.25	3.91	6.30	4.79	2.55	4.20
All	7.09	9.34	2.37	3.69	5.68	4.42	2.53	4.08

[a]IBRD includes IDA.
[b]IDB includes FSO.
[c]Argentina, Brazil, and Mexico.
[d]Chile, Colombia, Peru, Uruguay, and Venezuela.
[e]All other countries of Latin America.

Source: IDB.

Amortization and interest were generally payable in the currency of the borrower, although the latter was allowed an option to effect payment in the currency lent.[7] The IDB took the view, however, that Mexico and Venezuela were in a position to make payment for amortization and interest in the currencies lent--that is, generally in dollars.

Where payments in local currency were involved, these had to be made in amounts corresponding to the dollar equivalent, as in the case of ordinary loans in local currency, noted earlier. Thus, the responsibility for maintaining the value of local currency payments in terms of dollars, as well as the exchange risk with respect to loans in other currencies, was borne by the borrower.

In general, up until 1971, FSO maturities varied between fifteen and thirty years, according to the nature of the project, although loans for preinvestment and technical assistance were given shorter maturities. The grace period was fixed on the basis of the time taken to complete the project and other factors relating to the project and the financial situation of the borrowing country. In practice, FSO grace periods normally did not exceed four and one-half years.

Two important policy changes were made in 1970 in connection with the replenishment of FSO resources. First, it was agreed that the IDB would strengthen its existing policy of giving its least developed members priority access to the FSO. This was to be accompanied by the assignment of a larger proportion of ordinary capital resources to the relatively more developed countries. Second, it was decided to change the basis for repaying FSO loans. The Board of Executive Directors indicated that it

consider it desirable to establish the payment of amortization in the respective currencies loaned on new loans to be authorized from the Fund for Special Operations. As a consequence of the above, and in order to maintain the concessionary character of the

FSO, a general review of the terms and
conditions of these loans will be made with
regard to rates of interest, grace periods
and amortization periods, with a view to
minimizing the impact on the projects as
such and on the balance of payments of the
beneficiary countries.[8]

Insofar as the foregoing policy changes implied
giving the least developed member countries priority
access to the FSO, they were a movement in the right
direction. During the 1960s, there were a number of
anomalous cases in which low-income countries received a below-average per capita inflow of loans
from the FSO, whereas some countries with above-aver-
age incomes did much better.

The reason for this was the double criterion employed in assessing eligibility for FSO loans, so
that certain types of projects were regarded as
qualifying for FSO resources, as well as certain
types of countries (namely, the low-income countries).
Thus, the IDB was providing loans on easy terms not
only for the medium-income and low-income countries
but, also, for the high-income countries, with respect to social projects or projects that yield their
return only over relatively long periods.

If soft funds have to be rationed, the terms of
lending should, as a general principle, be determined by the over-all economic situation of a country
and not by the gestation period or other characteristics of individual projects. For the object of
soft terms is to reduce the proportion of disposable
foreign-exchange resources that has to be set aside
for debt service and thereby increase the resources
available for the financing of import requirements.

Clearly, it is the poorest countries, experiencing difficulties in mobilizing domestic savings or
in financing essential import needs, that should enjoy priority access to soft loans. This is true even
if the particular project to be financed is expected
to yield a high rate of profit and to generate larger
exports or reduce the need for imports. In cases of

high profitability, funds may be made available to the ultimate borrower on terms that reflect the expected rate of return.[9] But the fact that a particular project in one of the least developed countries generates a high rate of return does not mean that that country should be called upon to transfer the same amount abroad in the form of debt service as it would if it were in a higher-income group. For the capacity of the country to invest and to import is necessarily affected by the amount of any resources that have to be set aside for payment of amortization and interest on the sum borrowed.

Similarly, the character of particular projects--such as whether or not they are revenue-producing--should not determine the extent to which soft resources are made available to middle- or high-income countries. If there were unlimited soft resources available, there is no reason why the relatively more advanced countries should not have access to them, since it is just as true of them as it is of the least developed countries that the larger the amounts that they have to repay by way of debt service the smaller the resources remaining for investment or imports.

It is worth recalling that most of the funds made available to Western Europe under the Marshall Plan took the form of grants, not loans, notwithstanding the relatively high incomes of the European countries; it was decided, in effect, that the most efficient way of bringing about a given net transfer of resources to Europe would be through grants-in-aid, which would not impose any subsequent burden on the incomes or balances of payments of the recipient countries at a later stage of their recovery process.

Thus, a perfectly sound and respectable case could be made for providing easy borrowing facilities even for the higher-income countries in Latin America; and it will, in fact, be suggested below that there is no reason why the multilateral institutions should not provide grants, as well as loans, to developing countries.

But, in a situation where soft resources are strictly limited, as they are for the IDB, the method

whereby those resources are distributed among countries should depend on the over-all economic situation
of each country and not on the particular projects
submitted for financing. Just as the ultimate borrower in a low-income country may pay a rate of interest higher than that charged to the financial
intermediary by the IDB, so, also, would it be possible for the government in a high-income country to
provide local subsidies in cases where the rate of
interest charged by the IDB was considered high in
relation to the revenue-producing prospects of a
particular project.

Although the new FSO terms are expected to involve lower interest rates and longer grace and amortization periods than hitherto, this does not imply
an easing of terms. It is impossible to compare repayment in local currency with repayment in convertible currency--no matter what terms are applied in
each case--unless some assumption is made concerning
the circumstances, if any, in which local currencies
repaid might have to be made convertible.

On almost any plausible assumption, however,
repayment in convertible currency implies harder FSO
terms, even after allowing for lower interest rates
and longer periods of grace and amortization. The
new FSO terms may come close, in the case of the
least developed Latin American countries, to those
offered by IDA--namely, a service charge of .75 per
cent per annum and a maturity of fifty years, including a grace period of ten years.

The principal areas of activity for the FSO during the 1960s were agriculture and rural development,
particularly social aspects; urban development, particularly housing, sanitation, and other services
required in programs of integrated community development; and the promotion of education and technical
training. In addition, the FSO financed projects for
economic and directly productive infrastructure,
wherever FSO funds were considered appropriate for
this purpose.

So far as directly productive projects are concerned, the IDB has hitherto lent only to small- and

medium-scale industry and agriculture through financial intermediaries, such as national development
banks. In such cases, the benefits of the easy terms
have had to be passed on to the final borrowers, to
the greatest extent possible.

SOCIAL PROGRESS TRUST FUND

The character and purpose of the SPTF were described in Chapter 3, above, where it was noted that
the SPTF received resources of $525 million from the
United States, which were almost entirely committed
by the end of 1965, when it was decided to incorpor-
ate the activities of the SPTF into the FSO. In
1967, the decision was taken to use resources yielded
by service on SPTF loans to acquire participations
in FSO loans.

Terms and conditions were soft and sufficiently
flexible to accomplish the purpose of the loans. In
general, interest rates varied between 2 per cent
and 3.5 per cent, including a service commission of
.75 per cent payable in dollars. Both amortization
and interest were payable in local currencies or the
currencies lent, at the option of the borrower.
Maturities varied between fifteen and thirty years.
Grace periods were relatively short. No commitment
commission was charged.

It was provided that financial assistance from
the SPTF should be accompanied by effective self-
help and the allocation of appropriate resources by
the borrowing country to the objectives encompassed
by the loan program. The entire cost of a project,
including local costs, however, was eligible for financing by the SPTF, provided that the project in
question was part of a larger program involving adequate contributions by the borrowing country. No
restriction was applied to the financing of local
costs in foreign exchange.

POLICIES AFFECTING THE USE
OF OTHER RESOURCES

The Funds established by Canada, the Federal
Republic of Germany, Norway, Sweden, the United Kingdom, and the Vatican generally provide soft loans.
The Canadian Fund, which is the largest (60 million
Canadian dollars), provides two basic sets of terms:
interest-free loans with a maturity of fifty years
and a grace period of ten years (like IDA) and loans
carrying an interest rate of 3 per cent, a maturity
of thirty years, and a grace period of seven years.
In both cases, there is a service commission of .5
per cent to cover administrative costs. Service payments must be made in Canadian dollars. The Federal
German Fund ($9 million), which helps in financing
the rehabilitation of Bolivia's tin mines, makes
loans at an interest rate of 4 per cent per annum for
terms ranging up to ten years.

Of the resources committed under the United
Kingdom Fund,[10] 70 per cent are interest free. Maturities are fifteen to twenty-five years and grace
periods are up to seven years. An additional United
Kingdom Fund, established in 1971 on an untied basis,
charges interest at 3 per cent and provides for maturities of twenty-five years and grace periods of
four years.

The Swedish Fund applies an interest charge of
2 per cent, maturities of up to twenty-five years,
and grace periods of ten years. The Norwegian Fund
provides for an interest charge of 2 per cent, maturities of up to thirty years, and grace periods of
up to seven years.[11] The Vatican's _Populorum Progres-
sio_ Fund (amounting to $1 million) makes interest-
free loans with maturities up to fifty years and
grace periods determined by the IDB.

On loans from the Federal German, United Kingdom,
Norwegian, Swedish, and Vatican Funds, the IDB applies

a service commission of .5 per cent.   The resources
supplied by Norway, Sweden, and the Vatican are untied, as are the resources from the United Kingdom
Fund, set up in 1971, but the other funds are all
tied to goods and services produced in the respective
donor countries.

The Canadian International Development Agency
(CIDA) retains substantial control over the projects
financed under the Canadian Fund, and prior CIDA approval is needed before the IDB gives detailed study
to any proposed project.   CIDA must also approve any
loan contract before it is signed.   Consultation procedures are similar for the other Funds.

The establishment of these Funds, as well as of
the SPTF, is an interesting experiment in giving bilateral lending programs a multilateral character by
channeling them through an international agency.   The
price paid may be quite high in terms of operational
efficiency, however, since each Fund has its own particular features and requirements.   Moreover, the
normal delays that occur in the IDB processing of
projects are apt to be compounded by the additional
checks and cross-checks required in the case of the
above Funds.

The IDB has accepted responsibilities in relation to certain resources not directly under its control.   Such resources have been provided under agreements reached with the Export Development Corporation
(EDC) of Canada in July, 1965, and with the government of the Netherlands in September, 1965.   In the
case of the EDC, the agreement provided for parallel
loans by the IDB and the EDC on similar terms and
conditions and for independent loans by the EDC to
carry out projects proposed by the IDB.   Up to the
end of 1970, resources had been committed by the EDC
for an amount equivalent to $3.8 million.

A similar arrangement was reached with the government of the Netherlands, and resources equivalent
to $24.3 million had been committed under this pro-
gram by the end of 1970.   In both these cases, the
loans are made not by the IDB but by the EDC and the

government of the Netherlands. Nevertheless, the IDB
undertakes the important function of promoting, se-
lecting, and evaluating the projects to be financed.

THE CONCESSIONALITY OF
IDB LENDING

It was pointed out in Chapter 3, above, that the
terms on which the Latin American countries borrow
from the ordinary capital of the World Bank and the
IDB are determined not by considerations relating to
the debt-service position and available resources of
these countries but by factors arising out of the
economic policies pursued by the industrial countries
for the achievement of domestic objectives.

In recent years, the industrial countries have
become more and more reluctant to employ fiscal policy
for the containment of inflationary pressures. Although every opportunity afforded by periods of internal balance has been utilized in order to reduce
tax rates from levels regarded as excessive, there
has generally been strong resistance to tax increases
where demand pressures have built up. Much more emphasis, therefore, has had to be placed on increasing
interest rates as a means of limiting the demand for
new capital investment.

Since, for a variety of reasons, fixed investment
in the industrial countries has proved to be relatively insensitive to increases in interest rates,
the cost of borrowing has soared to almost unprece-
dented levels, without substantially easing the
stringencies in the capital markets. Thus, the high
level of interest charges that the developing countries have had to pay on loans from the World Bank
and the IDB are the result of the particular combination of fiscal and monetary policies that the industrial countries have selected in recent years, rather
than of factors pertaining to the situation of the
borrowing countries themselves.

Although a few of the Latin American countries
had made sufficient progress during the 1950s and

the 1960s to be able to pay market rates for funds
borrowed, most Latin American countries are in a much
less favorable position. They have good prospects
for economic growth and could make effective use of
supplementary resources from abroad over and above
domestic savings, but their export and debt-service
prospects are not such as to enable them to borrow
all they need on conventional terms or on the terms
on which ordinary resources are provided by the World
Bank or the IDB.

The foregoing remains true even after taking
into account the improvement in the debt structure
of Latin America that occurred during the 1960s.
This improvement was the result of the repayment by
several major debtors, notably Argentina and Brazil,
of much of their short-term debt; on the other hand,
the smaller Latin American countries added substantially to their indebtedness.

But, in the first place, it cannot be regarded
as desirable for countries such as Brazil and even
Argentina and Uruguay to be experiencing a resource
outflow at the present stage of their development.
Avramovic has estimated that, as a result of debt-
servicing obligations, these three countries sustained
a resource drain of $2.5 billion in the five years
from 1963 to 1967--which he calls a Marshall Plan in
reverse for these countries.[12]

In the second place, the ratio of debt service
due from Latin American countries in 1970 to debt
outstanding at the end of 1969 was 17 per cent. It
is true that this ratio represented an average of 12
per cent per annum for bilateral and multilateral
official lending, on the one hand, and over 23 per
cent per annum for private lending (including suppliers' credits, loans by private financial institutions, and bond flotations), on the other hand.[13]

But it should be noted that the degree to which
Latin American countries resorted to private financing at hard terms reflected, to a considerable extent, the shortage of official development funds in
relation to Latin America's capacity to make effective

use of them.   Thus, although Latin America accounted
for only one-quarter of the total debt of all developing countries to official bilateral and multilateral
institutions at the end of 1969, it was responsible
for one-half of the debt due to private creditors.

Moreover, even the 12 per cent ratio of debt
service to debt outstanding to official bilateral and
multilateral institutions reflects relatively hard
terms.   Avramovic considers that there is probably a
consensus that "the bench mark of 10 per cent on outstanding debt for the aggregate flow of amortization
and interest is a fairly stiff combination of terms
for development lending: this at least follows from
the discussions of the Development Assistance Committee of OECD in recent years."[14]

For example, a country whose debt had been contracted on a repayment schedule of twenty-five years
and an average interest rate of 6 per cent would be
servicing its obligations at the rate of 10 per cent
on the amount outstanding--4 per cent for amortization,
in addition to the 6 per cent for interest.   Such
terms are much harder than are those established by
the DAC countries as a standard for their own official lending.[15]   Yet, the average ratio of official
debt service to official debt outstanding in Latin
America in 1970 was significantly higher than the
bench mark of 10 per cent--itself much stiffer than
the DAC target for terms.   In these circumstances and
in view of the necessity for major recourse to borrowing from private institutions, it is not surprising that approximately one-fifth of Latin America's
export earnings have to be pre-empted for debt ser-
vice--a much higher ratio than can be regarded as
satisfactory in circumstances in which the prospects
for export earnings are quite uncertain in most
countries.

In his 1969 review, the Chairman of DAC published an indicator of the debt problem facing developing countries.   The indicator measures the ratio
of service on past external public debt, owed or
guaranteed by public authorities and falling due over
the next fifteen years, to the current (1967) value

of exports of goods and services. The ratio is calculated after deducting from the cumulative debt burden any excess of foreign-exchange reserves over two
months' import requirements.

The Chairman of DAC suggested that, when the already existing debt-service burden falling due within
the next fifteen years substantially exceeds the
value of current annual exports of goods and services,
this should normally be regarded as a warning that
serious debt difficulties could quickly arise in the
event of an unfavorable shift in the balance of payments. This indication would be particularly pointed
if a large volume of future borrowing were anticipated,
since the ratio given relates only to past borrowing.

The data provided by the Chairman of DAC are
shown in Table 9. As can be seen, more than half of
the Latin American countries (including all the South
American countries except Uruguay and Venezuela) have
debt ratios that indicate considerable vulnerability
to any unfavorable trend in the balance of payments.

Viewing the problem from another standpoint,
the Pearson Commission estimated that, in 1965-67,
the total amount of debt service paid on public and
private loans to Latin American countries was equivalent to no less than 87 per cent of the current flow
of new loans and that, if the flow of new lending
continued at the level of 1965-67 and on the same
terms, debt service would, by 1977, exceed new loans
by 30 per cent.[16]

In the circumstances described by the Chairman
of DAC and the Pearson Commission, it would appear
that the terms that the IDB is required to apply to
its loans, particularly loans out of its ordinary
resources, do not take sufficient account of the
debt-servicing capacity of its members. The harden-
ing of the terms of IDB ordinary loans during the
1960s reached the point at which IDB financing became
substantially less attractive to the private sector
in Latin America, especially if one takes into account
the exchange risk, which normally has to be borne by
the borrower.[17]

TABLE 9

Concessionality and Debt Burden

Country[a]	National Income per Capita in 1968 (in dollars)	Indicator of Debt Burden[b]	Grant Element of Grants and Loans in 1967[c] (in per cent)
Haiti	81	146	98
Bolivia	157	151	64
Paraguay	194	142	64
Ecuador	197	127	40
Honduras	223	56	63
Dominican Republic	238	107	73
El Salvador	246	36	36
Peru	246	143	40
Brazil	263	188	54
Guatemala	276	66	55
Colombia	299	155	53
Nicaragua	327	65	48
Costa Rica	384	119	64
Chile	449	181	32
Panama	507	33	35
Mexico	511	171	20
Uruguay	575	86	59
Argentina	779	146	37
Venezuela	803	1	18

[a]In ascending order of national income per capita in 1968.

[b]For description of indicator, see text.

[c]The grant element of a loan, which measures its degree of concessionality, is defined as the face value of the loan less the discounted present value of the future stream of amortization and interest, expressed as a percentage of the value of the loan. The discount rate applied is 10 per cent. Data include gross commitments of official grants and loans; guaranteed private export credits from DAC countries, as reported by the latter; and commitments from multilateral institutions.

Sources: U.N. Statistical Office for national income per capita; and OECD, Development Assistance, 1969 Review, Report by Edwin M. Martin, Chairman of DAC (Paris, December, 1969), for indicator of debt burden and grant element of grants and loans.

Moreover, the margin between the real cost of long-term financing from external and domestic sources probably narrowed in a number of the Latin American countries. Meanwhile, export credits provided by the industrial countries became more attractive, relatively, than capital provided out of the ordinary resources of the multilateral institutions, since the interest rate charged on these credits was generally lower than were the rates applicable to ordinary borrowing from the latter institutions.[18]

In addition, although the multilateral institutions still had the advantage of longer maturities, this advantage was narrowed by a lengthening of export-credit maturities. In any case, from the standpoint of the local entrepreneur, the cheapest funds were usually those borrowed from the official development finance institutions of his country, if available.[19]

As noted in Chapter 3, above, the Executive Directors of the IDB concluded in their report on the 1970 proposal for an increase in the Bank's resources that, in order to keep the lending rate "within tolerable limits," it would be necessary to increase the paid-in capital of the IDB. Further advances in interest rates would call for still larger amounts of paid-in capital, the use of FSO resources for interest subsidies on ordinary loans, or more flexible policies for mixing FSO and ordinary funds for particular projects, in order to establish a reasonable interest rate for the borrower concerned. Some of these solutions would necessitate amendment of the IDB Charter.

It would also be possible for the IDB, by a two-thirds majority vote, to reduce the 1 per cent rate of commission, and this is no doubt a measure that will commend itself to the Governors as soon as the Bank's reserves are considered sufficiently large. At the end of 1970, the IDB had a general reserve of $98.5 million against possible future losses and a special reserve of $25.6 million against liabilities created by borrowing. Thus, quite apart from the uncalled capital of the IDB, total reserves amounted

to $124.2 million, against a total funded debt of
$915.1 million.

The corresponding reserves of the World Bank
(which, as noted earlier, has not charged any commission since 1964) amounted to $1,444.2 million in
June, 1971, while the funded debt totaled $5,424.2
million. The World Bank's reserves, however, seem
extraordinarily large in relation to any probable
call upon them. It should be borne in mind that
the liabilities of both the World Bank and the IDB
are fully backed by the callable capital available
to them and that the IDB has undertaken not to assume
obligations in excess of the callable capital subscribed by the United States. A reduction in the
rate of commission would therefore not impair the
financial soundness of the IDB.

The cost of borrowing to the IDB, however, depends on the security rating given to its bonds by
the bond-rating services; it is thought that the
rating given to IDB bonds might be affected by any
policy change on commission charges. The fundamental
questions that are raised by soaring interest rates
in relation to the underlying Bretton Woods concept
of multilateral lending institutions are discussed
in Chapter 3, above.

                    LOCAL COST FINANCING

The IDB imposes no restriction on financing the
import component of a project, other than the restriction that requires the Bank, under normal conditions,
not to finance the entire cost of a project and to
comply with certain limitations placed on the origin
of goods imported.[20]

The IDB does, however, limit the extent to which
it is prepared to finance local costs, whether in
external or in domestic currency. This is in line
with a fundamental postulate of assistance policy,
according to which external resources should only
supplement domestic effort and initiative, and not
replace them. Only if there is an adequate local

effort will the borrower feel completely committed
to the success of a project and a sense of responsibility toward it.

The requirement for a local contribution of financial resources is also regarded as helpful in
stimulating efforts to mobilize such resources and
to channel them toward priority projects. Moreover,
the greater the local participation in IDB projects
over-all, the more widely will the IDB be able to
distribute its resources and the larger will be the
number of projects in which the Bank will be able to
carry out its task of institution-building and transferring skills and technology.

An additional factor tending to limit local financing by the IDB is the requirement that dollars
received for the financing of local costs must be
restricted to financing imports from the United States.
Such tying is not effective if the imports purchased
are such as the borrowing country would have purchased in the United States in any case. This is because tied purchases of this type release a corresponding amount of dollars that can be used freely
elsewhere.

If, however, the principle of "additionality"
is applied, so that countries are compelled to purchase goods that they would not otherwise have wanted
to import at all, an unfair burden is placed on the
recipient country. The United States has not applied
the principle of additionality to the use of funds
subscribed to the IDB,[21] and this means that the
requisite protection to the U.S. balance of payments
can be provided only if the financing of local costs
is strictly limited.

The policy of the IDB on the proportion of a
project to be financed from local resources varies,
depending on whether a project is in the public or
private sector and what resources are utilized. In
direct loans to the private sector, which are provided almost exclusively out of the ordinary capital
of the IDB, the general rule is that the applicant
should supply at least 50 per cent of the total cost

of the project. This rule may be modified if the
import component of the project is larger than 50
per cent of the total cost, in which case the IDB may
provide financing up to about two-thirds of the total
cost. The degree of development of the country concerned is also taken into account in determining the
local contribution.

Loans to the public sector out of the ordinary
resources of the IDB follow the same rule as do loans
to the private sector. Loans provided to the public
sector from the FSO, however, may embody more flexible
criteria. In the case of FSO loans to the least
developed countries of the region, the IDB has been
prepared, in some cases, to provide as much as 80
per cent of the cost of a particular project in foreign exchange. The rules for loans to development
banks and other financial intermediaries are similar
to those indicated above, but the proportion of external resources provided is calculated for the lending program as a whole rather than for each individual
project within the program.

LOCAL COST FINANCING
IN FOREIGN CURRENCY

The policy of the IDB on the financing of local
costs with foreign currency is governed, in the case
of ordinary loans, by certain restrictions imposed
in its Charter. According to the Charter, the IDB
may provide financing in the following ways:

(a)   By furnishing the borrower currencies
      of members, other than the currency
      of the member in whose territory the
      project is to be carried out, that are
      necessary to meet the foreign exchange
      costs of the project.

(b)   By providing financing to meet expenses
      related to the purposes of the loan in
      the territories of the member in which
      the project is to be carried out. Only
      in special cases, particularly when the

project indirectly gives rise to an
increase in the demand for foreign exchange in that country, shall the financing granted by the Bank to meet
local expenses be provided in gold or
in currencies other than that of such
member; in such cases, the amount of
the financing granted by the Bank for
this purpose shall not exceed a reasonable portion of the local expenses
incurred by the borrower.[22]

In applying the above provisions, the IDB divides
the foreign-exchange costs referred to under (a)
above into direct and indirect costs. Foreign-exchange costs are regarded as direct when they involve
the importation of goods not subjected to further
processing and embedded in the project or completely
used up in carrying out the project. Direct foreign-
exchange costs also include the cost of services of
foreign origin, notably the salaries of foreign consultants and engineers, and any interest payable in
foreign exchange during the construction period.
Foreign-exchange costs are regarded as indirect when
they result in the importation of raw materials and
components subjected to further processing. Also
included is the depreciation of imported machinery
and equipment utilized, but not wholly worn out,
during the project execution.

A third category of foreign-exchange costs that
may be regarded as attributable to a particular project are incurred as a result of a general rise in imports brought about by the additional wages, salaries,
and profits generated by a project and taking the
form of purchases of various types of goods, including
consumer goods, not related directly to the project.
These may be regarded as induced foreign-exchange
expenditure and are not included as part of the foreign-exchange component that may normally be financed
by the IDB with the foreign-exchange element included
in ordinary capital loans. These costs are regarded
as included in (b) above and only in exceptional circumstances will the IDB finance a reasonable portion
of such costs in foreign exchange.

The policy in respect to FSO loans is more flexible. Here, consideration is given to the economic situation of the borrowing country, its current and prospective balance-of-payments position, progress made in mobilizing domestic resources, and the likelihood that the project will generate resources in convertible currencies. FSO lending seeks, however, to avoid providing foreign exchange for financing local costs in a manner that would replace efforts to mobilize domestic resources.

No restrictions are applied to local cost financing with foreign exchange when the project concerned is in the field of agriculture or education. In the case of all other projects financed by FSO funds, the IDB has, since 1967, followed the policy of limiting the financing of local costs in dollars to 37 per cent of the total dollar financing authorized.

It must be recognized that these categories of direct, indirect, and induced foreign-exchange costs are defined in a manner that makes it possible to apply simple and practical rules for determining what the IDB will finance and what it will not. This is not to say that the definitions are without anomalies. Apart from the fact that there are restrictions on Bank financing of induced foreign-exchange costs, even though these are just as much part of the consequences of additional investment as are the direct and indirect costs, the major weakness of the definitions lies in the limitation placed on indirect costs.

In general, the more remote is an indirect cost from the project itself the less likely is it to qualify for Bank financing, even though the cost involved may be substantial. Clearly, any new project sets up a whole chain of indirect demands through its associated input requirements. Expanding the supply of such inputs may cause repercussions in plants that are several stages removed from the project in question.

As a practical matter, it would clearly be difficult to try and calculate the whole of the indirect import content of a particular project,[23] and this is

sufficient to account for the rules of thumb that
have to be applied. But this is only another way of
saying that project lending has severe drawbacks and
that a rational approach to the problem would necessitate authorizing the multilateral institutions to
undertake nonproject, as well as project, financing.

If the principle were followed that only the
direct and indirect import content of a project may
be financed by the IDB, it would mean that, where a
local enterprise was successful in bidding on part
or all of a project, IDB foreign-exchange financing
would have to be pro tanto reduced. This would discriminate against domestic industry, which it is the
object of external assistance to foster.

It should be borne in mind that a number of countries in Latin America have reached a stage of industrialization allowing them to produce a great variety
of capital goods. For example, it is estimated that
Brazil currently satisfies about 70 per cent of its
demand for industrial machinery from its own capacity.
Argentina, Mexico, and Chile, as well as a number of
other Latin American countries, have also made significant progress in the development of capital-goods
industries. This means that the import content of
investment projects in these countries is tending to
decline, so that a limitation on external financing
to the foreign exchange required for the financing of
imports would constitute a restriction tending to
have an adverse effect on the industrial development
of the countries concerned.

More generally, the above-mentioned principle,
taken literally, would tend to discriminate against
projects with low import requirements, even where
such projects were of the highest priority in terms
of broad development objectives. Low import requirements are, in fact, characteristic of projects in the
field of agriculture, education, and housing.

For these reasons, the IDB seeks to give a certain flexibility to its financing policies. Both for
ordinary and FSO operations, the IDB considers as expenditures in foreign currency any purchases of

capital goods from local industries, provided that
the purchases in question take place on the basis of
international tender, that the goods supplied by national industries have a domestic value added of not
less than 40 per cent of the total cost, and that
the price of the product in question is not more than
15 per cent higher than the lowest foreign bid.

The local price is, for this purpose, calculated
net of import duties and indirect taxes. The margin
of preference may be increased if the borrowing country can demonstrate the existence of exceptional circumstances, such as the availability of unused local
capacity. If the import duty applied by the borrowing country to a particular product is less than 15
per cent, the preferential margin is adjusted accordingly.

In carrying out this policy, the IDB has to try
to reconcile two objectives that may conflict to
some extent. On the one hand, it seeks to obtain
supplies for particular projects at the lowest possible cost. On the other hand, it cannot avoid taking a view of the broader implications of its lending
programs, and it is therefore reasonable for it to
pay prices somewhat higher than internationally competitive levels if, by so doing, it can provide an
additional stimulus to local capital-goods industries.

It may be noted that loans are generally authorized before the process of competitive bidding for
the projects to which they are allocated is undertaken.
At the time a loan is made, the IDB provides foreign
exchange for all purchases that will be subject to
international tender even though, as a result of the
tender, the orders may ultimately be placed with domestic industry. Regarding disbursements in local
currency that are not necessarily opened to international tender, the IDB follows various practices, depending on the character of the project and the source
of funds utilized.

Reference was made earlier to the policy of limiting the financing of local costs in foreign exchange
to 37 per cent of the total external resources pro-

vided--a policy designed to minimize the impact on
the U.S. balance of payments. For the purposes of
this policy, the term "local costs" does not include
indirect costs in foreign exchange as defined above.
Although the limit of 37 per cent was supposed to be
applied to the total lending of the FSO (excluding
loans for education and agriculture) in each calendar
year, the Board of Executive Directors has, in practice, tried to avoid exceeding this percentage in any
one project.

The result is that the FSO has operated well
within the 1967 limit--the actual percentage for the
covered sectors in loans authorized in 1969 was under
20 per cent. Even if agriculture and education are
included, less than 25 per cent of FSO foreign-cur-
rency loans authorized in 1969 were for local costs,
as may be seen from Table 10.[24] If the source utilized is one of the various special funds entrusted
to the IDB by nonmember countries, the financing of
local costs is, in general, rather limited, and depends on the provisions governing the fund in question.

Although the IDB, therefore, has a certain area
of discretion in making foreign exchange available
for financing local costs, its flexibility in this
respect is now distinctly less than it used to be
when the SPTF was active during the earlier years,
since there were no restrictions on the use of SPTF
resources in financing local costs.

Meanwhile, the attitude of the World Bank toward
financing local costs has tended to become more liberal,[25] so that IDB practice is now more closely in
line with World Bank practice. The more restrictive
policies now followed by the IDB with respect to
projects previously financed from SPTF resources has
had a particularly significant effect on IDB activity
in such fields as sanitation and housing, and this
is partly responsible for the decline in IDB lending
in these categories.

The excessive emphasis placed on local financing
of local costs creates a dilemma for the multilateral
agencies. They now recognize that, if they are rigid

TABLE 10

Financing of IDB Projects, 1969
(In Per Cent)

Source	Ordinary Capital	FSO	Total
Total cost of projects (in million dollars)	448.7	853.4	1,302.1
Local contribution	54.4	51.7	52.6
IDB loans	45.6	48.3	47.4
Direct imports	30.5	16.0	21.0
Indirect imports	10.5	10.9	10.7
Local costs financed with foreign exchange	4.2	6.9	6.0
Total loans in foreign exchange	45.2	33.8	37.7
Local-currency loans	0.4	14.5	9.7

Source: IDB.

in confining their financing to the import content
of projects, they may find themselves supporting
capital-intensive projects with the highest possible
import content, even though national priorities and
the best use of domestic resources might suggest a
different choice.

On the other hand, if they introduce a limited
measure of flexibility, involving some kind of formula or target for local financing, other kinds of
distortion may arise. For, as soon as it is provided
that a certain fixed proportion of local expenditure
may be financed with foreign exchange, an incentive
is created to maximize receipts of what is, in effect,
free foreign exchange by choosing those projects in
which the import content is lowest relative to the

foreign exchange supplied. Here, again, there is no
reason why the particular projects favored in this
way should necessarily be the best projects to choose
from the standpoint of national priorities.

As has already been pointed out, part of the
reason for the rapidly expanding share of agriculture
in IDB financing may well be that, since the cessation of the independent operations of the SPTF, which
had complete flexibility in local cost financing, it
is agricultural projects that offer the greatest
scope along these lines, because no restriction is
imposed on the financing of the local costs of such
projects. Agricultural projects are undoubtedly of
high priority, but it seems doubtful whether the degree of priority should be determined in this manner.

Although the foregoing dilemma cannot be avoided
entirely, the dangers of serious distortion of investment and import patterns would be smaller if
lending agencies discarded any kind of fixed formula
for local cost financing and simply stood ready to
finance local costs, wholly or partly, in a completely
flexible manner depending on circumstances.

The Pearson Commission recommended "that aid-
givers remove regulations which limit or prevent contributions to the local costs of projects, and make
a greater effort to encourage local procurement
wherever economically justified."[26] In the latter
context, it noted that the 15 per cent preference for
local suppliers granted by the World Bank had had
little practical effect, although there was substantial idle capacity for the production of many kinds
of capital goods in developing countries. This would
suggest the need for substantially increasing the
margin of preference granted, as well as for special
measures including provision of finance, if necessary,
to strengthen the domestic industries capable of
furnishing supplies for World Bank and IDB projects.

There is also much to be said for the idea that,
in order to promote the industrial development and
integration of the Latin American economies, it would
be advisable for the IDB and the World Bank to extend

to all Latin American producers, within the framework
of regional integration arrangements, the margin of
preference on bidding for projects that they currently
grant to producers in the recipient countries.

LOCAL COST FINANCING
IN LOCAL CURRENCY

Local currencies have been acquired by the IDB
through subscriptions to the ordinary resources of
the Bank and to the FSO. They have also been used
for payment of amortization and interest on FSO and
SPTF loans. As noted earlier, the IDB Charter requires that the value of currency holdings of the
Bank be maintained--that is to say, that

> whenever the par value in the International
> Monetary Fund of a member's currency is re-
> duced or the foreign exchange value of a
> member's currency has, in the opinion of
> the Bank, depreciated to a significant ex-
> tent, the member shall pay to the Bank
> within a reasonable time an additional
> amount of its own currency sufficient to
> maintain the value of all the currency of
> the member held by the Bank in its ordinary
> capital resources, or in the resources of
> the Fund, excepting currency derived from
> borrowings by the Bank. The standard of
> value for this purpose shall be the United
> States dollar of the weight and fineness
> in effect on January 1, 1959.[27]

In case of appreciation of a currency, the IDB must
return the appropriate amount of a member's currency
to it.

The above maintenance-of-value provisions apply
to subscriptions to the paid-in capital of the IDB
and to the FSO. They do not apply to local currencies held by the IDB for the SPTF as a result of
repayments. Maintenance of value of currencies borrowed from the FSO (other than dollars and the currencies of nonmember countries[28]) is the responsibility of the borrower.

Local currencies are used by the IDB for loans
to the respective member countries and to defray
part of the Bank's administrative expenses in these
countries. No restriction may be placed by any member on the use of its currency for making payment
for goods and services produced within its territory.[29]
A member's currency may also be used for payments in
any other country unless the member notifies the IDB
that it does not wish this to be done.[30]

Guatemala and Mexico invoked the latter restriction during the early days of the IDB, and the United
States requested the application of the same restriction in 1964 and subsequently, in connection with
new funds subscribed by it to the FSO. A similar
restriction had been applied to SPTF from the very
beginning. Although Latin American countries other
than Guatemala and Mexico did not formally request
any limitation on the use of their currencies, the
IDB has thus far used them only for local procurement
in the respective countries; however, the currencies
of six countries have been made available for local
cost financing in other countries, as indicated below.

There is no restriction on the proportion of
local expenditure that can be financed by the IDB in
the borrowing country's own currency, other than the
requirement that, in general, the IDB should finance
only part of the cost of a project; however, the use
of IDB holdings of local currency does not, of course,
add to the real resources available to the borrowing
country for financing new investment. The IDB has
therefore adopted the policy that, no matter what
the nature of a project may be, the local currency
supplied by the Bank should not exceed 50 per cent
of the total amount lent. As shown in Table 10, the
average local currency component of FSO lending in
1969 was 30 per cent.[31]

It is considered possible that the limit on the
local currency component may be raised at some time
in the future, because of the large amounts of local
currency coming into the hands of the IDB. It may
even be argued that, in the least developed countries,
where domestic resources may be particularly difficult

to mobilize, there is a case for having all the local
expenditures associated with particular projects
financed out of the local currency holdings of the
IDB. This would mean, in effect, that certain projects in the least developed countries might, in the
future, be held to qualify for 100 per cent financing
by the IDB, import costs being financed out of the
external resources of the Bank and local costs out
of its local currency holdings.

This procedure would enable the IDB to move more
quickly and more decisively in the least developed
countries than it is able to do when local effort and
local resources have to be marshaled effectively.
It implies, however, a degree of IDB freedom and
autonomy in implementing particular projects that
might not always be welcome to the host country.
Moreover, such an arrangement would result in an ab-
normal debt/equity ratio for the enterprises concerned
and would go counter to the IDB principle that the
borrower should indicate his commitment to the ven-
ture by placing some of his own resources at risk.

OTHER USES OF LOCAL CURRENCY

As noted in Chapter 3, above, the governments
of Argentina, Brazil, Mexico, and Venezuela agreed,
in 1967, that part of their contributions to the FSO
should be made available to cover local costs in
other countries, in addition to financing exports
under IDB projects from the above-mentioned countries.
In 1970, Chile and Colombia agreed to a similar
arrangement.

In implementing the 1967 agreement, the IDB
Board of Executive Directors decided that one-half
of the contributions of the four specified countries
might be used for loans to other Latin American
countries, two-thirds being set aside for financing
exports from the respective contributing countries
and the remaining one-third being used for financing
local costs in the borrowing country under FSO
projects.

Local cost financing was to be arranged by the
IDB, in agreement with the monetary authorities of
the contributing and the borrowing countries, in such
a way as to ensure that the currency loaned would
not be converted into other currencies. Service payments on the loans were to be made in the currencies
loaned, or, at the election of the debtor, in his
own currency, except that loans in Mexican pesos or
Venezuelan bolivares were to be serviced in the currencies disbursed.

There had not yet been time, by the end of 1970,
for the above arrangements for making use of the currencies of the four (and, more recently, six) countries to yield significant results.[32] In the absence
of preferential treatment, it was no doubt difficult
for the four countries to supply project requirements
at prices and qualities that borrowing countries
would find attractive; and, as far as the financing
of local costs was concerned, the arrangements required to ensure that the currencies loaned would
not be converted into other currencies probably involved various administrative complexities.

A new departure, in 1970, was the negotiation
of an agreement between the IDB and the government
of Argentina, whereby the latter was to provide special funds in its own currency to help finance projects in the neighboring countries of Bolivia, Paraguay,
and Uruguay. These funds, which were in addition to
contributions made by Argentina as a member of the
IDB, were designed to help provide the local counterpart contributions for IDB-financed projects in the
three countries. The first loan under this arrangement was made late in 1970; it amounted to $1.2 mil-
lion in Argentine pesos and was extended to Uruguay
for a joint project across the Uruguay River connect-
ing the two countries.

THE FUTURE OF LOCAL-CURRENCY
FINANCING

Over the coming years, the IDB will be receiving
much larger additions to its holdings of local cur-

rencies, through the servicing of FSO loans, than it
is likely to be able to use effectively. The local
administrative expenses of the IDB cannot absorb more
than a small proportion of these funds, and the number of cases in which local currencies could, or
should, be used for loans to the respective issuing
countries is rather limited.

Where a country has effective banking institutions under central direction or control and there
is reasonable monetary stability, it does not have
to be lent its own currency by the IDB. Indeed, an
IDB loan to a borrower in the currency of his own
country may be troublesome from the standpoint of
over-all monetary balance. If such a loan is consistent with the monetary policy and investment priorities of the borrowing country at the time of disbursement, it is unnecessary, because the same funds could
have been made available by the domestic banking
system.

If such a loan is inconsistent, it tends to
thwart the policies of the country concerned and to
add to domestic inflationary pressure and, hence, to
pressures on the balance of payments. Moreover, in
view of the relatively long time that normally elapses
between the authorization and the disbursement of
IDB loans--measured in years, rather than in months--
it is quite possible for a loan in the borrowing
country's currency that appeared quite consistent
with over-all monetary stability at the time it was
authorized to become a source of difficulty by the
time it is disbursed.

One possible objective in lending a country its
own currency would be to try to achieve, thereby, an
additional degree of control over the project in
question and over the performance of the borrowing
entity, over and above the control resulting from
the provision of resources in the form of foreign
exchange. This is not, apparently, one of the objectives of the IDB in this respect. Borrowing countries might well resist external surveillance and
control in direct proportion to the share of their
own currency in the total resources provided.

Local-currency lending by the IDB may have advantages where there are institutional obstacles to
loans from domestic financing agencies or where there
is a situation of rapid inflation. In some cases,
an enterprise may be unable to borrow locally, even
though it has a sound project, owing to the limited
domestic facilities available. It is particularly
difficult to secure local financing on a long-term
basis under conditions of strong inflationary pressure, since there is usually no established means
whereby the lender can be protected against the effects of rapidly rising prices. In cases such as
these, IDB local-currency loans, with their provision
for maintenance of the value of interest and principal in terms of dollar equivalents, may play a useful
role.

The decision that the servicing of future FSO
loans should be in the currency disbursed, principally dollars, will limit new inflows of inconvertible
currency into IDB holdings, but it will not solve the
problem of the existing holdings or of the service
on past FSO/SPTF loans. The origin of the difficulty
lies partly in the fact that the multilateral institutions have not, in general, been authorized to
make grants to member countries for project financing.[33] Consequently, FSO and SPTF resources were
provided partly in the form of loans to be serviced
in the domestic currencies of the respective borrowers. A better solution might have been to make grants
to these countries, rather than loans, although this
would not have helped as far as subscriptions to the
paid-in capital and the FSO were concerned. It could
be argued that it might have been better to limit
such subscriptions to whatever countries could afford
in convertible currency, rather than to create an
artificial structure based on inconvertible and, for
the most part, unusable currencies. If, however,
subscriptions to the IDB had been limited to convertible currency, there would have been a lesser sense
of participation by the Latin American countries, if
only for psychological reasons.

Moreover, it is to be hoped that, in due course,
an increasing number of Latin American countries may

be able to supply project inputs to their neighbors
against their own currencies loaned to the latter by
the IDB. There is, therefore, a case for a pragmatic
solution to the problem--on the one hand, maintaining
the present system for subscriptions, at any rate
for the time being, while, on the other hand, convert-
ing into grants those portions of FSO/SPTF loans authorized prior to 1971 and repayable in domestic
currencies only.

The objection to grants for project financing is
that the inducement to the recipient to make effective
use of scarce resources is considerably weakened
thereby. This consideration, however, applies to the
enterprise receiving the funds and not necessarily
to the government of the country in which the enterprise is located. It would be entirely possible to
adopt a two-step procedure whereby resources were
made available to a government in the form of a grant
and were passed on by the government to domestic enterprises as loans on appropriate terms as regards
interest, maturity, and grace period. Such a procedure would avoid the fiction of local-currency repayment and, hence, the piling up of inconvertible
currencies by the IDB, while maintaining the pressure
for financial responsibility on the part of the ultimate borrowers.

PROTECTION OF THE U.S.
BALANCE OF PAYMENTS

Far-reaching arrangements have been undertaken,
since 1964, to minimize the impact of IDB operations
on the balance of payments of the chief source of
capital--the United States. This contrasts sharply
with the policies of the World Bank Group, which provides loans both from the World Bank itself and from
IDA on a completely untied basis. Borrowers from
the World Bank are generally required to obtain goods
and services through international competitive bidding by suppliers, which may be located in any of
the World Bank's member countries or in Switzerland.
As a temporary accommodation to the United States,
however, it was agreed among the contributing coun-

tries to IDA on the occasion of that agency's second
financial replenishment that, for procurement in
other countries, the resources supplied by the United
States would be the last to be drawn upon.

Prior to 1964, IDB lending from its ordinary
and FSO resources was subject to the same rules that
apply in the case of the World Bank and IDA. Only
the resources of the SPTF were subject to restriction--
these could be spent only for the purchase of supplies produced in the United States, in the borrowing
country, or, when advantageous to the borrower, in
other member countries of the IDB.

When the resources of the FSO were expanded in
1964, the United States, as noted earlier, made use
of the right conferred on member countries of the
IDB by its Charter and restricted the use of dollars
made available under the new contribution in the manner already applicable to the SPTF.[34] Moreover, a
special letter of credit procedure was instituted
to ensure that dollars disbursed for local currency
expenses would be used only for purchases in the
United States.

The United States also informed the IDB that
loan contracts involving the use of dollars from its
additional FSO contribution should stipulate that at
least 50 per cent of the gross tonnage of equipment,
materials, and goods financed from that contribution
should be transported in U.S.-registered ships, provided that such ships maintained tariffs regarded as
fair and reasonable for merchant ships operating under the U.S. flag.

The restrictions applied on the origin of imports had the effect of raising the cost of goods
financed by FSO loans. As a result of these measures,
only about $185 million of the $2.3 billion contributed to the FSO by the end of 1970 were available
for untied procurement. Furthermore, in 1967, as
noted earlier, limitations were placed on FSO financing of local costs in foreign exchange. The effect
of tying on the cost of FSO procurement was less
serious than it might have been, insofar as borrowing

countries could pay their debt service in local currency; however, the new provision adopted in 1970,
whereby FSO loans will have to be serviced in convertible currency, may cause difficulty unless this
is accompanied not only by an easing of terms but,
also, by untying.

CHARACTER OF EXPENDITURE
FINANCED

The IDB will finance any of the component expenditures of a project, with the exception of two
particular items: the administrative costs of the
borrower during the period of execution of the project and expenditures on working capital. As regards
the first of these, the control of such expenditures
presents difficulties for an external agency, and,
since the sums involved are generally in local currency and of relatively small amount, they can be
readily financed from the local contribution. Working capital likewise involves expenditure in local
currency that can often be financed by the borrower.

Notwithstanding these considerations, certain
exceptions have been made in connection with agricultural projects financed with FSO or SPTF funds. One
example of such projects is the provision of credit
to small farmers. Generally speaking, small farmers
in Latin America engage in the production of food-
stuffs on a scale not requiring large investments of
fixed capital. The demand for fixed investment is
particularly limited where the farmer does not own
the land that he cultivates. In such cases, the IDB
has agreed to finance from FSO or SPTF resources the
purchase of such goods as fertilizers, insecticides,
and seeds, where such expenditure is part of a properly worked-out program. This is a program of considerably importance to the agricultural development
of Latin America.

PROVISION OF GUARANTEES

Although its Charter enables the IDB to provide
guarantees, the IDB did not make use of this authority

during its first ten years, for reasons similar to those that prevail in the case of the World Bank.[35] If the IDB were to provide a guarantee for a loan to a member country or for a bond flotation by that country, it would, in effect, be creating an obligation against callable capital, just as if it had made a loan itself. Thus, the exercise of guaranteeing authority by the IDB would not add to the total resources available to member countries.

At the same time, the provision of guarantees would involve considerable costs for the IDB, since it would have to go through the same process of evaluation as it would if the IDB were itself lending the money and would not be able to recover the costs involved except by charging a commission, which would be disadvantageous for the borrowing country concerned. On the whole, it appears that the cost of borrowing is likely to be less where the IDB itself makes the required loan, and, to this extent, the interests of the IDB and of its members point in the same direction.

It could be argued that, by guaranteeing bonds issued by Latin American countries in the capital markets of developed countries, the IDB could assist in developing a receptivity in those markets, thereby helping to restore the standing and creditworthiness of the borrowing countries. This, in turn, might make it possible, in the longer run, for such countries to go to the capital markets on their own, without IDB guarantees. It is, however, open to question whether the matter would develop in this way, and it appears just as likely that capital markets would begin to regard an IDB guarantee as an indispensable feature in bonds issued by Latin American countries--even by those that have hitherto been able to raise funds without such guarantees.

NOTES

1. Exceptionally, in the case of the financing of intraregional exports of capital goods, the rate has been maintained at a level of 6.5 per cent, so as not to frustrate the whole purpose of such financing.

2.   The IDB has followed the practice of charging
the .5 per cent special commission on 40 per cent of
the foreign exchange lent and not on the remaining
60 per cent. As a result, at the end of 1969, the
average cost to the borrower of the foreign-exchange
component of loans out of the ordinary resources of
the IDB, including both interest and service commission, came to 8.19 per cent, while loans in local
currency carried a charge of 8 per cent.

3.   Loans to finance intraregional exports of
capital goods had shorter maturities.

4.   The spread of terms between the more developed and the less developed countries would be shown
as even greater than indicated in Tables 6-8 if allowance were made for the fact, discussed below, that
FSO loans, which form a larger proportion of total
IDB lending to the latter than to the former countries, have thus far generally been repayable in
local currency.

5.   IDB, Agreement, Art. IV, Sec. 1.

6.   A commitment charge on the unused portion
of loans begins sixty days after the signing of the
contract. This charge, which amounts to .75 per cent
for economic projects and .5 per cent for social
projects, is payable proportionately in dollars and
in any other currencies laid down in the loan contract.

7.   This option is sometimes exercised because
of relatively unfavorable exchange rates applied at
certain times to particular currencies. For example,
in some countries with dual or multiple exchange
rates not recognized by the FSO, borrowers have been
able to gain an advantage by repaying in dollars
purchased at the official rate.

8.   IDB, Proposal for an Increase in the Resources of the Inter-American Development Bank (Washington, D.C., April, 1970), par. 5.06.

9.   In practice, the interest differential thus
generated in local currency is channeled into a devel-

opment fund that, after consultation with the IDB, may be used by the government to carry out other priority projects or to cover local contributions to projects financed by external resources.

10. Commitments to the end of 1969 totaled £3 million, and the remaining £1 million of the amount originally allocated was then incorporated into the ordinary capital of the IDB in the form of a direct loan.

11. The Swedish Fund amounts to the equivalent of $5 million and the Norwegian Fund to $2 million.

12. Dragoslav Avramovic, "Latin American External Debt," Journal of World Trade Law, Vol. 4, No. 2 (March/April, 1970), 142.

13. See World Bank/IDA, Annual Report 1971 (Washington, D.C., 1971), p. 52.

14. Avramovic, "Latin American External Debt," p. 131.

15. Thus, for example, the terms target adopted by DAC in 1969 established certain standards of concessionality for official development assistance. Examples of loans of the required concessional standard are: 25 years maturity, 7 years grace period, 2 per cent interest; 30 years maturity, 8 years grace period, 2.5 per cent interest. See OECD, Development Assistance, 1969 Review, Report by Edwin M. Martin, Chairman of DAC (Paris, December, 1969), Annex III.

16. Partners in Development: Report of the Commission on International Development [Pearson Commission] (New York: Praeger, 1969).

17. All direct loans from the IDB to private borrowers require that the value of repayments be maintained in terms of dollars. In the case of global loans, national development institutions may have various policies--in some cases, requiring maintenance of value, in others, not. In countries with depreciating currencies, if the maintenance of value

obligation is not required of subborrowers, high interest rates are charged.

18. During 1969, for example, export credits
typically carried interest rates of 5.5-7 per cent,
as against the 8 per cent charged by the IDB on its
ordinary lending from April, 1969.

19. See T. Graydon Upton, Executive Vice-President of the IDB, in Felipe Herrera and others, Una
Década de Lucha por América Latina (Mexico D.F.:
Fondo de Cultura Económica, 1970), pp. 242-43. [Here-
after referred to as Década.]

20. Restrictions placed on the origin of imports
depend on the type of resources used by the IDB in
each case. In general, imports financed out of the
ordinary capital of the IDB may be obtained from any
member of the IMF, as well as from Switzerland, provided, in the case of industrial countries, that the
exporting country has been declared eligible by virtue of having supplied cumulative resources to the
IDB in excess of cumulative orders received from the
Bank. Imports financed by FSO loans may be obtained
from the United States or any member of the IDB,
provided, in the latter case, that the IDB has given
the necessary authorization. Purchases against loans
provided from funds supplied by Norway, Sweden, the
United Kingdom (1971), and the Vatican are untied,
but the other special funds are tied.

21. The United States applied this principle to
its bilateral assistance program, however, until 1970.

22. IDB, Agreement, Art. III, Sec. 6.

23. A rough approximation could be attempted in
cases where an up-to-date input-output table was
available in sufficient detail.

24. If, however, the financing of indirect foreign-exchange costs were included in the concept of
local costs, the percentage would rise to over 50,
as shown in Table 10.

25. The World Bank's Annual Report 1963-64 referred to the Bank's intention of financing local expenditures on high-priority projects in cases where such projects would not receive adequate support if financing were limited to the cost of direct imports. IBRD/IDA, Annual Report 1963-64 (Washington, D.C., 1964), p. 8.

26. Partners in Development, pp. 176-77.

27. IDB, Agreement, Art. V, sec. 3 (a).

28. Dollars were excluded because the dollar is the basic unit for valuation of the assets of the IDB, and nonmember currencies were exempted because the IDB obtains them without assuming responsibility for maintaining their value.

29. IDB, Agreement, Art. V, sec. 1 (a).

30. Ibid., Art. V, sec. 1 (c).

31. Table 10 shows that IDB loans financed 48.3 per cent of FSO projects in 1969, of which 14.5 per cent, equivalent to 30 per cent of total FSO lending, consisted of local currency loans.

32. Colombia received a small loan of approximately $26,000 in Mexican pesos in June, 1970.

33. Part of the technical assistance provided by the IDB and the World Bank and all of the technical assistance provided by the United Nations Development Program (UNDP) are in the form of grants. The multilateral agencies do not, however, make grants for projects that yield revenue or even for social projects in such fields as education. The World Bank, however, has stated that "IDA could . . . give grant aid." IDA, 50 Questions and Answers (Washington, D.C., May, 1970), p. 3.

34. IDB, Agreement, Art. V, sec. 1 (c).

35. Ibid., Art. III.

OVER-ALL ACTIVITY

The volume of loans approved by the IDB rose
from an average of $200-300 million during the first
four years of operations to a level of over $600 mil-
lion a year in 1969-70, as shown in Table 11. It is
hoped that lending volume may increase to an annual
rate in the vicinity of $900 million by 1973 if de-
cisions taken at the end of 1970 on the replenishment
of resources are implemented. Soft lending from the
FSO currently accounts for about two-thirds of the
total volume of loans authorized, and it is expected
that this proportion will be maintained during the
years ahead. The average size of IDB ordinary loans
in 1970 was of the order of $11 million and that of
FSO loans was $12 million. This compared with an
average of $24 million per loan from the World Bank
and $11 million for IDA credits.

The increase in IDB lending to Latin American
countries has not sufficed to offset the decline in
the flow of resources from the United States, as
may be seen in Table 12. Since the sharpest decline
in AID activities in Latin America took place in
program lending, the shift from AID to the IDB as a
channel for U.S. official funds was accompanied by a
fall in the share of program lending and a rise in
the share of project lending.

TABLE 11

Loans Approved, by Funds, 1961-70[a]
(In Million Dollars)

Year	Ordinary Capital	FSO	SPTF	Other	Total
1961	115.1	45.1	112.1	--	272.3
1962	78.6	41.1	202.8	--	322.5
1963	166.5	33.9	46.7	--	247.1
1964	150.5	46.8	84.5	--	281.8
1965	118.7	196.0	48.6	4.4	367.7
1966	87.6	290.8	--	2.6	381.0
1967	168.3	305.8	--	13.2	487.3
1968	197.7	206.6	--	28.4	432.7
1969	208.6	412.5	--	10.7	631.8
1970	194.4	443.0	--	7.0	644.4
Total	1,486.0	2,021.6	494.7	66.3	4,068.6

[a]Amounts net of cancellations as of December 31, 1970.

Source: IDB.

The trend in World Bank lending is not clear from Table 12, but the President of the World Bank has indicated his intention to double financing by the three World Bank Group institutions in Latin America during the period 1969-73, compared with the preceding five years. During the fiscal years 1970 and 1971, World Bank Group lending to Latin America averaged some $750 million a year, and it is expected that this amount will be exceeded in the fiscal year 1972; this suggests that the goal for 1969-73 may be exceeded.

An examination of the figures in Table 13 shows that, up to the end of 1970, the IDB had authorized

TABLE 12

Latin America: Credits Authorized by Selected Official Sources, 1961-69
(In Million Dollars)

Source	1961	1962	1963	1964	1965	1966	1967	1968	1969
Development credits and grants	1,302.4	1,283.4	1,129.3	1,384.5	1,385.0	1,527.7	1,624.0	1,851.9	1,491.5
U.S. Government	733.0	605.8	559.9	949.8	625.4	791.6	961.7	842.5	503.4
AID total	375.0	422.3	472.0	708.5	460.2	638.5	483.1	409.2	360.3
AID grants	104.2	116.7	145.7	91.6	116.5	128.6	88.2	80.7	78.2
AID project and sectoral	212.8	139.1	244.3	294.4	190.7	219.9	179.6	193.6	222.1
AID program	58.0	166.5	82.0	322.5	153.0	290.0	215.3	134.9	60.0
EXIMBANK	358.0	183.5	87.9	241.3	165.2	153.1	478.6	433.3	143.1
World Bank	276.5	348.8	307.3	135.4	384.0	342.1	166.5	578.5	385.1a
IBRD	206.8	328.0	303.7	103.3	371.1	322.6	156.8	551.4	339.3
IFC	10.7	9.4	--	9.1	9.4	12.0	7.7	9.1	34.1a
IDA	59.0	11.4	3.6	23.0	3.5	7.5	2.0	9.1	11.7
IDB	292.9	328.8	260.1	299.3	375.6	394.0	495.8	430.9	637.1
Ordinary capital	129.2	83.7	179.4	164.0	123.6	98.8	170.3	193.6	214.5
FSO	48.1	40.2	33.6	49.4	196.6	291.3	313.1	210.1	412.5
SPTF	115.6	204.9	47.1	85.9	51.2	--	--	--	--
Other	--	--	--	--	4.2	3.9	12.4	27.2	10.1
Food for peace	101.4	222.8	215.4	263.3	145.6	139.4	141.1	156.3	137.0
Compensatory aid	1,048.2	348.9	352.6	312.1	476.1	467.9	391.4	428.8	219.4
U.S. Treasury	147.0	125.0	60.0	96.3	69.8	12.5	75.0	4.8	--
IMF	456.2	221.3	166.2	142.7	258.0	331.5	316.4	424.0	219.4
EXIMBANK	445.0	2.6	126.4	73.1	148.3	123.9	--	--	--
Total	2,452.0	1,855.1	1,697.3	1,959.9	2,066.7	2,135.0	2,156.5	2,437.0	1,882.0

aData for IFC relate to fiscal year 1970 and include loan of $10 million to ADELA Investment Company

Source: CIAP, Evaluation of Latin American Development in 1969 and Estimates of Resources Required in 1970/72, Document CIAP/435 (Washington, D.C., August 26, 1970).

loans to a total value of $4,068.6 million, against which it had disbursed $2,152.6 million. This appears to imply an average time lag of three to four years between authorizations and disbursements,[1] as may be seen by comparing the cumulative disbursements in each year against the level of cumulative authorizations attained three years earlier, as follows (in million dollars):

Cumulative Authorizations		Cumulative Disbursements	
Year	Amount	Year	Amount
1961	272.3	1964	404.4
1962	594.8	1965	586.3
1963	841.9	1966	798.4
1964	1,123.7	1967	1,040.8
1965	1,491.4	1968	1,331.5
1966	1,872.4	1969	1,724.9
1967	2,359.7	1970	2,152.6

It should be borne in mind that disbursements against individual loans are normally spread over a substantial period of time, ranging generally from three to five years, depending on the character of the project and the length of time required for its execution.

Apart from time lags resulting from the inherent characteristics of particular projects, borrowers have sometimes experienced difficulties in meeting the conditions laid down in the respective loan contracts and in project programing and management. The IDB Group of Controllers has commented that "on occasions the conditions imposed on the borrowing countries have been beyond their capacity to meet."[2] This does not necessarily imply that the conditions were unreasonable, but, rather, that some borrowers are unused to the standards of business performance and accounting required by the international lending agencies. This has made it necessary for the IDB to give assistance in meeting these standards.

The rate of disbursement could probably be improved substantially if it were possible to undertake

TABLE 13

Loans Authorized and Disbursed, and Repayments, 1961-70[a]
(In Million Dollars)

Year	Annual		Cumulative		Cumulative Ratio (in per cent)	Repayments	
	Authorized	Disbursed	Authorized	Disbursed		Annual	Cumulative
1961	272.3	6.6	272.3	6.6	2.4	--	--
1962	322.5	58.7	594.8	65.3	11.0	.4	.4
1963	247.1	141.0	841.9	206.3	24.5	1.6	2.0
1964	281.8	198.1	1,123.7	404.4	36.0	6.7	8.7
1965	367.7	181.9	1,491.4	586.3	39.3	13.3	22.0
1966	381.0	212.1	1,872.4	798.4	42.6	35.2	57.2
1967	487.3	242.4	2,359.7	1,040.8	44.1	46.5	103.7
1968	432.7	290.7	2,792.4	1,331.5	47.7	62.6	166.3
1969	631.8	393.4	3,424.2	1,724.9	50.4	80.6	246.9
1970	644.4	427.7	4,068.6	2,152.6	52.9	106.7	353.6

[a]Amounts net of cancellations as of December 31, 1970.

Source: IDB.

a simplification of the complex legal and other procedures involved in complying with the terms of loans.
But any such simplification remains difficult so
long as the international community expects the multilateral agencies to operate with an absolute minimum
of risk and so long as the actions and decisions of
these agencies have to stand up to the judgment of
investors in long-term bonds.

The ratio of disbursements to authorizations
has been somewhat higher for the ordinary capital
resources of the IDB than for the various soft-loan
facilities combined, as shown in Table 14. This is
a reflection of ordinary loans not having risen as
fast as have FSO loans and the average time lag between authorization and disbursement tending to
lengthen when lending activity accelerates.

Moreover, many of the projects financed by the
FSO, especially in the social field, raise unfamiliar
problems in the course of execution, calling for
careful examination, whereas projects financed out
of the ordinary capital resources of the IDB are usually much more straightforward and conform to a well-
established pattern. Thus, for example, power projects normally raise far fewer difficulties than do
projects for agrarian reform or urban development.
Finally, the FSO caters particularly to the least
developed countries, which tend to have greater difficulty in meeting the conditions imposed in loan
contracts.

DISTRIBUTION BY COUNTRIES

Table 15 gives an analysis of the intercountry
distribution of lending by the IDB. It will be seen
that close to one-half of IDB loans have gone to Argentina, Brazil, and Mexico, which was to be expected
because of the size and the population of these countries. On a per capita basis, Brazil and Mexico fall
well below the average,[3] whereas Paraguay, Nicaragua,
Costa Rica, Uruguay, Panama, and Chile head the list,
in that order.

TABLE 14

Cumulative Authorizations and Disbursements,
by Source of Funds, December 31, 1970[a]
(In Million Dollars)

Source	Cumulative Authori- zations	Cumulative Disburse- ments	Ratio (in per cent)
Ordinary capital	1,486	893	60
Other	2,583	1,260	49
FSO	2,022	752	37
SPTF	495	493	99
Other	66	16	24
Total	4,069	2,153	53

[a]Amounts net of cancellations as of December 31,
1970.

Source: IDB.

Indications are that the most important factor
governing the distribution of IDB resources was probably, as in the case of the World Bank, the availability of suitable projects. Of the eleven countries
with per capita incomes of less than $300 in 1965,
only three--Bolivia, Honduras, and Paraguay--received
per capita inflows of more than $20 from the IDB over
the period 1961-70 as a whole. Conversely, of the
eight countries (other than the recent members, Jamaica and Trinidad and Tobago) with per capita incomes over $300 in 1965, all except Mexico received
inflows of over $20 per capita, and, in five of them,
the figure was in excess of $30 per capita. Although
the IDB has sought to give particular attention to
the preinvestment activities required to generate
suitable projects in the developing countries, the
effort has thus far brought about only limited results.

TABLE 15

Distribution of Loans, by Countries, 1961-70

Country[a]	Loans (in million dollars)	Distribution (in per cent)	Distribution Per Capita (in dollars)	National Income Per Capita in 1965[b] (in dollars)
Haiti	12.3	.3	2.6	76
Bolivia	102.1	2.5	21.3	123
Ecuador	109.7	2.7	18.6	184
Paraguay	98.2	2.4	42.4	190
Brazil	875.6	21.5	9.5	193
Honduras	55.0	1.4	22.1	205
Peru	224.3	5.5	17.0	218
Dominican Republic	58.9	1.4	14.1	221
El Salvador	49.6	1.2	14.9	233
Colombia	374.7	9.2	18.3	246
Guatemala	79.4	2.0	15.8	260
Nicaragua	75.4	1.9	39.6	309
Costa Rica	61.5	1.5	36.2	330
Mexico	531.5	13.1	10.9	412
Jamaica[c]	10.9	.3	5.6	414
Chile	297.9	7.3	31.1	419
Panama	48.5	1.2	34.3	425
Uruguay	99.8	2.4	35.0	574
Trinidad and Tobago[d]	8.9	.2	8.6	585
Argentina	549.6	13.5	22.9	728
Venezuela	269.0	6.6	26.8	733
CABEI[e]	65.4	1.6	4.5	f
ADELA[g]	10.4	.3	f	f
Total	4,068.6	100.0	15.5	340

[a]In ascending order of national income per capita in 1965.
[b]Year 1965 represents midpoint of period covered.
[c]Jamaica did not join IDB until 1969.
[d]Trinidad and Tobago did not join IDB until 1967.
[e]Central American Bank for Economic Integration.
[f]Not applicable.
[g]ADELA Investment Company.

Sources: IDB and U.N. Statistical Office.

The low-income countries fared somewhat better
in the distribution of resources from the FSO, considered separately.[4] This was to be expected since
the FSO, as the soft-loan facility of the IDB, should
presumably give priority to these countries. Even
here, however, as previously pointed out, there are
a number of anomalous cases in which low-income countries received a below-average per capita inflow of
loans from the FSO, and vice versa. In 1970, the
Board of Executive Directors decided to "place
strengthened emphasis on granting soft loans to the
relatively less developed countries" and to "assign
first priority" to their requirements.[5]

SECTORAL DISTRIBUTION

The sectoral distribution of IDB lending over
the entire period from 1961 to 1970 is shown in Table
16. It will be seen that agriculture, industry, and
mining have absorbed over 40 per cent of IDB lending;
electric power, transportation, and communications
have taken a further 31 per cent; and social development projects involving water supply and sewage systems, urban development and housing, and education
have accounted for nearly 25 per cent of the total.
A relatively small amount of funds has gone into
preinvestment and export financing, although these
aspects of IDB activity are much more important than
the proportion of resources devoted to them would
appear to suggest.

The sectoral distribution of IDB funds represents
a marked contrast with the traditional pattern of
multilateral lending. Up until the early 1960s,
electric power and transportation accounted for 90
per cent of the World Bank's lending activity in
Latin America. At the time when the IDB was beginning
its operations, only 10 per cent of new bilateral and
multilateral aid commitments combined were being directed to the agricultural sector, and, within this
10 per cent, a major proportion was going into irrigation, which, in many cases, was more in the nature
of agricultural infrastructure than a direct stimulus
to production. The IDB's emphasis on the expansion

TABLE 16

Sectoral Distribution of Loans, 1961-70

Sector	Cumulative 1961-70 Amount (in million dollars)	Per-centage	1961 Per-centage	1965 Per-centage	1970 Per-centage
Agriculture	1,066.3	26.2	16.8	9.1	36.7
Industry and mining	620.6	15.3	29.1	17.7	7.3
Export financing	53.2	1.3	--	.1	1.9
Subtotal	1,740.1	42.8	45.9	26.9	45.9
Electric power	577.7	14.2	6.3	8.5	16.0
Transportation and communications	685.1	16.8	.8	30.9	25.2
Subtotal	1,262.8	31.0	7.1	39.4	41.2
Water supply and sewage systems	486.2	12.0	23.3	21.5	4.5
Urban development and housing	350.8	8.6	22.9	7.7	4.5
Education	150.4	3.7	--	1.8	2.1
Subtotal	987.4	24.3	46.2	31.0	11.1
Preinvestment	78.3	1.9	.8	2.8	1.8
Total[a]	4,068.6	100.0	100.0	100.0	100.0

[a]Details do not necessarily add to totals because of rounding.

Source: IDB.

130

and modernization of Latin American agriculture and
industry and on social development projects reflected
important innovations in international assistance
policy.

The difference between the sectoral distribution
of World Bank and IDB loans was in part associated
with the large proportion of IDB loans that were made
to private enterprise, either directly or indirectly,
through national development institutions in the borrowing countries. This was possible for the IDB because it did not need governmental guarantees in all
cases, but was empowered to accept guarantees by
private banks or development corporations. For the
World Bank, however, governmental guarantees were
indispensable, except with respect to the relatively
limited operations of the IFC. Thus, the World Bank
was compelled to limit its lending mainly to governmental entities, such as the public corporations responsible for power and transportation in the Latin
American countries.

The above considerations were, however, merely
a reflection of a more fundamental issue. Infrastructure provided the main focus of the lending activity of the World Bank during the early postwar
years because it did not raise some of the difficult
problems associated with the financing either of
productive enterprise, on the one hand, or of social
projects, on the other hand. Loans to productive
enterprise would have satisfied the requirement that
the projects financed by the World Bank should yield
an adequate rate of return, but they would have
raised other questions.

For example, the question would always arise,
in such a case, about whether capital was available
from private sources. If it was, the view would be
taken that the World Bank ought to reserve its resources for other projects. If the proposed project
had not succeeded in attracting private capital,
there might be reason to doubt whether the enterprise
was really likely to be profitable.

Serious doubts were also entertained about
whether an institution such as the World Bank should

get involved in projects requiring a high degree of
familiarity with the local business community and
local market conditions. The World Bank appeared
better equipped to handle large-scale loans, such as
those required for infrastructure projects, rather
than the much smaller financing requirements of nu-
merous private farmers or industrial entrepreneurs.
Since, in any case, infrastructure was a priority
requirement for development, it seemed that projects
of this type, especially power projects, offered a
most convenient and effective means for transferring
external resources.

The objection to social projects, on the other
hand, was that these were regarded as not coming
within the scope of basic or directly productive activities that would have the effect of expanding the
growth potential of the borrowing countries concerned.
It was felt that, insofar as countries could afford
such projects at all, they ought to undertake them
out of their own resources and not make use of scarce
international capital for this purpose.

The IDB played a vital role in bringing about a
change in traditional thinking on these matters.
Latin American countries certainly benefited from
the building up of infrastructure brought about by
the World Bank. But a point was bound to be reached
at which the development of infrastructure might
move ahead of the productive capacity required to
make effective use of the new power and transportation facilities created. Thus, the Latin Americans,
in campaigning for the establishment of the IDB during the 1950s, laid particular emphasis on the need
for a regional development bank that would have the
power to lend to private agriculture and industry
without government guarantee, as noted in Chapter 1,
above.

In order to overcome the difficulties in seeking
to lend directly to small and medium-sized farmers
and industrialists, the IDB channeled substantial
resources through national development banks and
other specialized lending agencies in the Latin American countries. Chile and Mexico were among the

first Latin American countries to establish national
development banks, but the number of such institutions
in Latin America grew rapidly during the 1960s with
the active encouragement of the IDB.

By the end of 1969, IDB lending to the private
sector in Latin America reached a total of $942 mil-
lion, equivalent to a little more than one-quarter
of the over-all lending volume of the IDB. Of this
amount, $154 million (16 per cent) took the form of
direct loans to privately owned corporations, while
the remaining $788 million (84 per cent) were chan-
neled through financial intermediaries. In view of
the overhead costs involved, direct loans are not
usually made in amounts of less than $1 million ($.5
million in the case of the smaller countries). Loans
to financial intermediaries have averaged approximately $6 million, but some have been much larger
than this, and some much smaller.

Similarly, the IDB was influential in helping
to bring about a reappraisal by the international
community of the role of social projects in development. In the course of that reappraisal, it came to
be understood that expenditures on education should
be regarded as being in the nature of investment in
human capital--rather than of consumption, as had
been thought hitherto--and that better housing,
health, sanitation, and water supplies may contribute
at least as much to productivity as do transportation
facilities.

SECTORAL CHANGES IN FINANCING

In the course of the 1960s, the earlier differences between the sectoral pattern of lending of the
World Bank and the IDB were substantially narrowed
as a result of World Bank entry into the financing
of agricultural, industrial, and social projects and
the initiation of a number of IDB projects in the
fields of power and transportation. The effect of
these developments may be seen in Table 17. It will
be noted that electric power, transportation, and
communications now account for rather similar propor-

TABLE 17

IDB and World Bank: Sectoral Distribution of Lending, 1968–69[a]

Sector	IDB Amount (in million dollars)	IDB Per-centage	IBRD[b] Amount (in million dollars)	IBRD[b] Per-centage
Agriculture	277.2	26.1	780.2	19.2
Industry and mining	93.5	8.8	533.5	13.1
Transportation and communica-tions	269.9	25.4	1,300.6	32.0
Electric power	246.2	23.2	907.1	22.3
Water supply and sewage systems	63.9	6.0	67.1	1.6
Urban development and housing	37.3	3.5	--	--
Education	35.8	3.4	161.7	4.0
Preinvestment	14.8	1.4	18.1	.4
Export financing	23.7	2.2	--	--
Other	--	--	302.0[c]	7.4
Total	1,062.3	100.0	4,070.2[d]	100.0

[a]1968/69–1969/70 for World Bank.
[b]IBRD includes IDA.
[c]Industrial imports, 200; loan to IFC, 100; and family planning, 2.
[d]Details do not add to total because of rounding.

Sources: IDB and World Bank annual reports.

134

tions of the total lending activity of the IDB and
the World Bank, while the World Bank has actually
overtaken the IDB with regard to the proportion of
its lending devoted to industry.

The proportion of total resources devoted by
the World Bank and the IDB combined to electric power
and transportation in 1968-69 seems rather large and
is probably larger than is the share of these sectors
in the total investment outlays of the Latin American
countries. Indeed, the current lending structure of
the multilateral institutions appears to be vulnerable
to one of the arguments used by the Latin American
countries in calling for the establishment of the IDB
during the 1950s--namely, that industry was being
starved in favor of infrastructure.

Although the management of the IDB does not appear to anticipate any major change in the pattern
of IDB lending during the 1970s,[6] it seems unlikely
that the present distribution of loan activity would
be maintained if considerably larger resources were
made available to the multilateral lending institutions, in line with the recommendations of the Pearson Commission.

The shift to infrastructure has been accompanied
by a considerable increase in the average size of
IDB loans. At the outset of its operations, it was
felt that, until the IDB had gained the confidence
of those supplying its resources, it should, so far
as possible, avoid giving loans for amounts larger
than $5 million. By 1970, however, the average size
of loans had risen to $11 million, and a number of
individual loans had exceeded $35 million.[7]

The share of agriculture in IDB lending has also
increased--from approximately 17 per cent and 22 per
cent of total financing in 1961 and 1962, respectively, to over 36 per cent in 1970. This has resulted partly from a growing recognition of the
importance of this sector in economic development
but largely, also, from the IDB not restricting the
financing of local costs in the case of agricultural
projects using FSO resources. Whether such inter-

sectoral differences in the proportion of local cost
financing are calculated to encourage the best possible pattern of IDB lending is open to question.
It is true that the IDB could not have been effective
in assisting the agricultural sector if it had not
been prepared to finance local costs, since the import content of agricultural projects tends to be
low. As suggested in Chapter 4, above, however,
there is a strong case for not tying aid to imports
in any sector.

A steep decline has taken place in the proportion of IDB financing devoted to social projects,
notably in the fields of sanitation and housing.
Indeed, the latter two categories alone accounted
for about 46 per cent of total financing in 1961 and
nearly 54 per cent in 1962. More recently, projects
of this type have declined in absolute terms, and
even more so in relative terms. By 1970, sanitation
and housing accounted for only 9 per cent of the
total volume of lending by the IDB.

Part of the reason for the emphasis on social
projects during the early years was the fact that
these were largely financed by the SPTF, established
by the United States within the framework of the IDB
precisely in order to encourage projects of this
type. Although it would have been possible, in
theory, for the FSO to provide resources for similar
projects, the interest of Latin American governments
in such projects had waned in the meantime, and an
important deterrent was the U.S. limitation on the
extent to which the IDB could finance local costs
with the dollars contributed to the FSO. Here again,
therefore, the question of local cost financing was
influential in affecting the structure of IDB lending.

The most surprising shift in the sectoral pattern of IDB lending, shown dramatically in Table 16,
was that affecting industry. In the first four years
of the IDB's existence, industry and mining accounted
for $280 million of IDB lending, equivalent to one-
quarter of the total. In 1964, IDB lending included
$100 million for industry and mining, corresponding
to over 35 per cent of the total authorizations for

the year. By 1970, not only had the proportion of
lending activity devoted to industry declined to less
than 8 per cent of the total but, also, the absolute
amount of lending in this field had fallen to only
$47 million.

The IDB was thus having difficulty in fulfilling
one of the basic objectives for which it had been
established in response to Latin American demands.[8]
The reasons for this development are discussed in
Chapter 6, below.

NOTES

1. Part of this lag corresponds to the time
taken for the negotiation of loan contracts; as noted
in Chapter 2, above, in the case of the IDB, these
negotiations take place after approval of the loan
by the Board of Executive Directors.

2. IDB, Group of Controllers of the Review and
Evaluation System, Study of Sources and Uses of Funds,
CRE 1/69-Rev. 2 (Washington, D.C., August, 1969), p.
41.

3. The low per capita flows to Trinidad and
Tobago and Jamaica, shown in Table 15, are a result
of these two countries not having joined the IDB until 1967 and 1969, respectively.

4. This accounts for the low-income countries
having received the softest terms, on average, as
noted in Chapter 4, above.

5. IDB, Proposal for an Increase in the Resources of the Inter-American Development Bank (Washington, D.C., April, 1970), par. 5.05.

6. See Felipe Herrera and others, Década, p. 59.

7. In 1970, the IDB made a loan of $66.5 mil-
lion to Brazil for the construction of an electric
power transmission network to carry power from Ilha
Solteira to São Paulo.

8.   This remains true even after taking into
account the resources provided for export financing,
which go entirely to industry and which accounted
for $12 million of IDB lending in 1970.   The addition
of this amount would still bring the share of industry in total IDB lending activity in 1970 to less
than 10 per cent.

6

LOANS FOR AGRICULTURE

One of the most notable contributions of the IDB to Latin American development has been its support of agriculture. Although the agricultural sector does not itself generally play a dynamic role in the development process, the economy as a whole cannot move forward if agriculture is not freed from traditional constraints. An examination of the history of both developed and developing countries shows clearly that agrarian reform has almost invariably been an indispensable element in the economic advance of those countries that now have the highest incomes.

The only exceptions are those countries, such as the United States, where the frontier of cultivation could be continually pushed back as the demand for agricultural products grew in line with income. In the European countries and Japan, however, this line of development was not possible, and economic growth therefore made it necessary to sweep away feudal and prefeudal systems that would otherwise have held back the general process of development.

Agriculture plays a key role, if for no other reason, because of its sheer size. In the great majority of Latin American countries, the share of agriculture in the total gross product is 20 per cent

or more, and, in a number of them, it is closer to
40 per cent; the share in employment is considerably
larger than this. It is important to overcome the
backwardness of this major sector in order to avoid
a widening of the gap between it and the industrial
and other sectors geared to the market economy.

Agriculture also has a critical function to perform in providing the marketable surplus of food that
other sectors, notably the industrial sector, need
for their sustenance. If the output of food rises
no faster than the needs of the rural population
that produce it, the only way in which the nonagricul-
tural sector can obtain adequate supplies will be
through imports from abroad. But, since the developing countries are rarely able to earn as much foreign
exchange as they need for their most essential imports of raw materials, intermediate products, and
capital goods, any spill-over of the demand for food
to the import sector can take place only at the expense of development goods.

Another reason for giving special attention to
the needs of agriculture is that this sector provides
a very large part of the market for domestic industry.
Although the developing countries are now paying more
attention to the possibilities of export markets for
manufactured goods than they did in the past, the
experience of the industrial countries provides ample
demonstration that thriving export industries are
usually built on the foundations provided by a secure
home market. Particularly during the learning process
and the early stages of development it is the domestic market that must provide growing points for home
industry, and a prosperous rural community is therefore an indispensable condition for industrial advance.

The view that special efforts are required to
stimulate the development of agriculture must, of
course, be distinguished from another proposition
with which it is often confused--namely, the proposition that, since the comparative advantage of the
developing countries lies in agriculture (or so it
is asserted), it is to agriculture that the greatest

efforts should be directed, rather than to industry.
A high level of unemployment and underemployment on
the land, however, make it essential for other sectors of the economy to be developed at a rate that
would permit them to offer new employment opportunities to those who would be unable to find productive
work even if agriculture were reorganized on a more
rational basis.

Although there are a number of countries--such
as Australia, Canada, and Denmark--that have attained
high levels of income on the basis of agricultural
specialization, they also have highly developed industries and derive a relatively small proportion of
their income and employment from agriculture.[1] Thus,
it cannot be said, in the case of the developing
countries, that agricultural development should take
priority over industrial development but, rather,
that development in both sectors should go hand in
hand.

Up until 1960, Latin American agriculture received relatively little external assistance. Since
that time, there has been a major increase, and, as
may be seen from Table 18, the IDB has provided
nearly one-half of the resources, the remainder being
supplied mainly by the World Bank Group and by AID.[2]
In a number of countries, the IDB contribution has
been quite substantial in relation to government appropriations for agriculture. For example, on the
average, from 1961 to 1968, the IDB provided resources
equivalent to 10-12 per cent of government appropriations for agriculture in Chile and Colombia, 16-19
per cent in Mexico and Peru, and as much as 36 per
cent in Guatemala.

Agriculture also accounts for a major share of
total IDB lending. During the period from 1961 to
the end of 1970, about one-quarter of all IDB lending
was directed to specific agricultural projects. If,
in addition, account is taken of infrastructure
projects in rural areas (including rural housing,
rural water supply, roads, and power), as well as
technical assistance, training, and research associated with agriculture, the resources allocated by

the IDB to rural development in the widest sense
amounted to over one-third of total IDB commitments.

On the average, the IDB provides one-third of
the total costs of the agricultural projects that it
finances, the remainder coming from local resources.
This proportion is somewhat less than is the share
of the IDB in the financing of projects outside agriculture, because the import content of agricultural
projects tends to be significantly lower than that
of projects in other sectors.

The principal concern of the IDB is to help low-
income farmers to raise their levels of production
and productivity by providing both technical assistance and financial resources. Additional objectives
are to promote agricultural diversification, so as
to reduce dependence on a limited number of crops,
and to stimulate the expansion of regional trade in
agricultural commodities. The IDB estimates that,
from 1961 to 1969, more than 700,000 farmers benefited from indirect loans (through national financial
intermediaries) totaling $375 million, which implies
that the average size of loans was $535. Since a
large part of the assistance goes to low-income borrowers, most of the loans are on soft terms. Of the
total resources provided for agriculture from 1961
to 1969, 70 per cent were derived from the FSO (and,
during the earlier years, from the SPTF); in 1967-69,
this proportion rose to 80 per cent.

Table 19 shows that nearly one-third of IDB agricultural projects have been in the field of irrigation and drainage, while projects for general development and diversification have been almost equally
important. Almost all the activities listed, except
some of the irrigation and land-settlement projects,
contain a large element of rural credit to farmers;
about one-half of the total volume of lending has
taken the form of rural credit in one form or another.
Most of this credit has gone to small- and medium-
scale farmers to encourage diversification, technological improvements, land-settlement schemes, and so
forth. Part of the credit has also served to finance
working capital--such as fertilizer, seed, small

TABLE 18

External Assistance to Latin American Agriculture, 1961-68

Source	Total Commitments for All Purposes (in million dollars)	Commitments for Agriculture (in million dollars)	Share of Total Commitments (in per cent)	Share of Commitments for Agriculture (in per cent)
IDB	2,797.9	643.6	25.7	48.3
World Bank Group	2,733.0	350.1	25.1	26.3
AID	3,037.8	296.8	27.9	22.3
EXIMBANK	2,172.4	41.8	19.9	3.1
CABEI[a]	155.5	.3	1.4	[b]
Total	10,896.6	1,332.6	100.0	100.0

[a]Central American Bank for Economic Integration.
[b]Less than .1 per cent.

Source: IDB.

TABLE 19

IDB Loans to Agriculture, by Type, 1961-69

Type	Volume of Loans (in million dollars)	Share (in per cent)
Irrigation and drainage	265.4	31.2
General development and diversification	231.6	27.2
Mechanization and technological development	110.3	13.0
Land settlement	104.1	12.2
Livestock development and animal disease control	91.4	10.7
Marketing	35.2	4.1
Cooperative and community development	3.9	.5
Other	9.2	1.1
Total	851.1	100.0

Source: IDB.

tools, and insecticides. The Bank has been the major
external source of rural credit in Latin America.

Although IDB policy is to support agrarian reform, lending activities in support of such reform
have been rather limited; and the IDB has devoted
substantially larger resources to the colonization
of new areas than to the restructuring of old ones.
This is the result of the general backwardness of
Latin American countries in promoting adequate programs of land reform. Here, one comes up against a

fundamental difficulty (discussed in Chapter 7, below) --namely, that, if one takes the view that it is inappropriate for an external agency to bring pressure to bear on the policies of the various governments, this involves a necessary limitation upon the freedom of action of such an agency to insist on such policy changes as land reform.

One important example of IDB support of land reform is to be found in a $20 million loan to Chile as a contribution to a program to provide 30,000 land-reform beneficiaries with credit facilities. The total program amounts to nearly $300 million over a seven-year period. The beneficiaries are small farmers, who have been allocated between six and twenty hectares each and whose income before the reform was generally below $300 a year. The loans are channeled through new forms of communal or cooperative rural institutions operated by the beneficiaries themselves. The Bank also has helped to finance technical assistance related to land reform, as well as a number of studies on this subject. It has further provided assistance for the training of officials in the planning and implementation of land-reform programs.

There have been significant shifts in the direction of IDB activity in the agricultural field in recent years. One of the most important effects of the cessation of activity by the SPTF was that expenditures on land-settlement projects, financed mainly from these funds, declined. Offsetting increases have taken place in irrigation, which rose to account for almost two-fifths of total authorizations for agriculture in 1967-69. There was also a relative increase in resources devoted to livestock development.

A further change in composition is expected as the IDB begins to undertake new activities in connection with the development of forest resources and fisheries. Although it is estimated that Latin America has about 25 per cent of the world's forest reserves, the region imports over four times as much in the way of forest products as it exports; and it contributes only 1 per cent of total world exports of

TABLE 20

IDB Loans to Agriculture, by Purpose, 1961-69[a]

Purpose	Volume of Loans (in million dollars)	Share (in per cent)
Infrastructure[b]	291.0	39.5
On-farm inventory build-up[c]	206.9	28.1
On-farm improvement[d]	119.0	16.2
Processing and transport	54.6	7.4
Technical assistance and research	29.9	4.1
Other	34.6	4.7
Total	735.9[e]	100.0

[a]Data relate to sample of 114 agricultural loans.
[b]Roads, electricity, irrigation, storage facilities, farm housing, drinking water, and health and community centers.
[c]Farm machinery, livestock, fruit trees, and permanent pastures.
[d]Farm buildings, fencing, land clearing, and land improvement.
[e]Details do not add to total because of rounding.
Source: IDB.

these products. The IDB hopes to be able to promote both a more-rational process of tropical wood extraction, taking account of the need for conservation of tropical resources, and a program of reforestation with fast-growing varieties of soft woods.

The rise in the share of infrastructure projects in agricultural programs corresponds to a similar trend in the over-all lending programs of the IDB,

which was noted earlier. The shift was a deliberate
one, reflecting, in part, the view that the massive
resources available to the IDB were not used to
their best advantage by granting a large number of
very small loans, and that these resources could have
exerted a greater effect on agricultural investment
and output if a lesser number of more substantial
loans had been advanced to medium- and large-scale
farmers.[3]

The change was also motivated by the belief that,
in many cases, the margin between the interest
charged by the IDB and that paid by the subborrowers
may not have been sufficient to cover the administrative costs of the national development banks or
the amounts defaulted and that, consequently, these
operations may have been in the nature of a public
service subsidized by the national banks, whose financial structure may have been weakened thereby.[4]

But, the fact--if it is a fact--that the IDB
program of lending to small- and medium-scale farmers
has been accompanied by losses and defaults does not
necessarily mean that shifting to large-scale agricultural projects will provide a convenient way out.
The large-scale or commercial farmer does not really
need the IDB, for he can usually obtain whatever financial accommodation he requires from other sources.
It is the small and medium-sized farmer that needs
help, if really important progress is to be made in
developing Latin American agriculture.

Moreover, infrastructure projects are less
oriented to the direct stimulation of agricultural
development than those concerned, say, with supplying
farm machinery or processing facilities or with the
provision of rural credit. They provide facilities--
such as roads, electricity, irrigation, and storage--
that enlarge the capacity for growth, but they do
not necessarily stimulate growth itself. Infrastructure projects are also less easily focused on
the particular needs of small and medium-sized farmers unless the region in which they are deployed
happens to be a region of small and medium-sized
farmers only.

The selection of livestock projects, which are of increasing importance in the lending activity of the IDB, raises particular difficulties, because such projects may, in some cases, have the effect of bolstering a form of traditional agriculture and a pattern of land tenure that are unsuited to modern development needs; however, there is no doubt that major efforts are needed to overcome Latin America's protein deficiency and that livestock products also offer good export prospects.

OBSTACLES TO AGRICULTURE

Despite the stepping up of external assistance to Latin American agriculture during the 1960s, the rate of growth of agricultural production has been disappointing, averaging only 2.3 per cent per annum. Even if the production of export crops is excluded, the rate of growth of food production for domestic consumption averaged only 2.9 per cent per annum. Per capita food production was no higher in 1968 than in 1960.

One of the main obstacles to the development of Latin American agriculture has been the failure to bring about the structural changes that are needed. In 1965, less than 2 per cent of the active population held more than 50 per cent of the farm land, averaging 400 hectares per person, and received nearly 20 per cent of the agricultural income, averaging over $6,000 annually per economically active person. At the other end of the scale, the lower two-thirds of the agricultural population received only one-third of the agricultural income, averaging about $275 per economically active person, equivalent to less than $90 per head over-all;[5] and one-fifth of the active population held only 2.4 per cent of the land, corresponding to an average of less than two hectares per person. This maldistribution of land is the main reason for rural underemployment and inequitable income distribution. It has been estimated by ECLA that, in order to achieve a reasonable level of income--in the $700-800 range per economically active farmer--small landholders would need

five times the amount of land that they now hold.
In most countries, the additional land could be made
available from large estates that are now underutilized.[6] Although some governments have sought to provide additional land by the colonization of new
settlements, programs along these lines have been
found relatively expensive and are therefore slowing
down.

In the absence of reform (except in a handful
of countries, notably Chile and Peru), there is a
growing employment crisis in agriculture. It was estimated, in 1968, that the number of unemployed in
rural areas in Latin America amounted to more than
10 million persons of working age, equivalent to
about one-third of the economically active population
in the agricultural sector.[7] Moreover, even after
allowance for the rising trend in the migration of
workers out of agriculture, it is estimated that the
total rural labor force will grow by about 1 million
workers annually.

A basic problem for the IDB during the 1970s,
therefore, is how to deal with a situation in which
neither the agricultural nor the industrial sectors
are providing sufficient employment even to make
inroads on existing unemployment, let alone provide
work opportunities for the new entrants into the
labor force.

INDUSTRY

From 1961 to the end of 1970, the IDB lent $621
million to the industrial and mining sectors of Latin
America, which was equivalent to 15 per cent of the
total funds committed by the Bank for all purposes.
About one-third of this total was made up of direct
projects, while the remaining two-thirds were channeled through national development banks. Apart
from project aid to industry, the IDB also made
available $53 million for the financing of capital-
goods exports to the Latin American region. Clearly,
these are very small sums in relation to the industrial investment requirements of the Latin American

economy. They are also small in relation to IDB
resources; by contrast, nearly 40 per cent of total
financing by the Asian Development Bank has been devoted to industry.[8]

Over 80 per cent of the funds supplied to industry by the IDB have come out of its ordinary resources, reflecting the view that industry ought to be
sufficiently productive to borrow on the Bank's normal terms.[9] More than 75 per cent of the funds allocated have gone into chemicals, base metals, and
paper, and these, together with the cement and food-
processing industries, have accounted for over 90
per cent of IDB industrial financing. Only 3 per
cent of the total has gone into metal products. Although IDB industrial lending thus appears to have
followed a distinct pattern, no deliberate sectoral
priorities have been set by the Bank.

One reason for the very limited activity of national and international lending agencies in the
field of industry is the belief that industrial investment is best undertaken by private capital,
which has access to the world's capital markets and,
therefore, does not need assistance except in special
cases. An additional factor is a reluctance to see
public enterprise enter the industrial arena in developing countries on the grounds that governmental
agencies or corporations are apt to lack the flexibility and dynamism needed to cope with the rapidly
changing industrial scene--in which risk-taking and
innovation are important elements in success and
technological progress and obsolescence put a premium
on the capacity for rapid adaptation.

Mention was made, in Chapter 5, above, of the
decline in the volume of IDB industrial financing in
the course of the 1960s. It is worth noting, however,
that the share of industry in the total inflow of
loans into Latin America actually increased considerably over this period--from 10.6 per cent of the
total in 1961 to 16.3 per cent in 1967.[10] As may be
seen from Table 21, this was because the decline in
IDB lending for industry was more than offset by an
increase in lending from EXIMBANK.

TABLE 21

Industrial Loans, by Selected Agencies, 1961-67
(In Per Cent)[a]

Source	1961	1964	1967	1961-67
IDB ordinary capital	39.4	35.9	27.7	34.6
FSO	11.4	5.2	10.2[b]	6.0[b]
Subtotal	50.8	41.1	37.9	40.6
EXIMBANK	43.0	48.1	56.5	44.0
AID	3.1	10.9	5.7	9.4
IBRD[c]	3.1	--	--	6.1
Total	100.0	100.0	100.0	100.0

[a]Details do not necessarily add to totals because of rounding.
[b]Includes SPTF.
[c]IBRD includes IDA.

Source: OAS, External Financing for Latin American Development, OEA/Ser. H/X.14, CIES/1382 (Washington, D.C., May, 1969), Table I-4.

In December, 1969, the IDB contracted for the services of a private consulting company known as ADELATEC to do a study of industrial financing requirements in Latin America. In the course of its study, ADELATEC sought an explanation for the drop in IDB financing of industry.[11] ADELATEC pointed out that, in the case of the IDB's indirect loans, much of the difficulty was due to the restrictions imposed by the Bank on the use of funds by financial intermediaries. At least 50 per cent of a project must be financed out of local resources.

IDB funds cannot be used to buy stock, grant convertible loans, finance working capital, buy land, or refinance debts or deferred assets. Rather, IDB resources must be used basically to finance imported fixed assets. The object of these restrictions is to ensure that there is adequate local support and that IDB funds will be used primarily for direct imports. The result of the restrictions, however, is that it takes an average of four years from the signing of a loan document for disbursements to be completed. The most restrictive factor in this regard has been that of obtaining domestic resources to finance working capital and long-term local expenses.[12]

In addition to these delays and difficulties, there has been strong competition among the industrial countries in the financing of their commercial exports. Consequently, although the cost of borrowing from the ordinary resources of the IDB has been severely affected by rising interest rates in the industrial countries, the terms of suppliers' credits have not. Thus, the average interest charge on loans from EXIMBANK rose only from 5.75 per cent in 1961 to 6 per cent in 1969, whereas the cost of borrowing from the ordinary resources of the IDB went up from 5.75 per cent to 8 per cent. The lengthening of the maturities of suppliers' credits further reduced the advantages of borrowing from the IDB.

Even greater difficulties have been experienced in direct lending to industry, mainly because of the complex process of evaluation, the loan conditions imposed, and limitations on financial flexibility. Exposed to the constant scrutiny of its members and always conscious of the need to maintain the highest possible credit rating in capital markets, the IDB makes the most cautious and exhaustive evaluations of industrial projects, involving a protracted period of approval.[13] This, however, is a procedure unsuited to many industrial projects, where the time factor may be critical and risk is unavoidable.

At the same time, the IDB requirement for a governmental or bank guarantee is something that few companies are able or willing to meet. This, again, involves serious delay, since the guaranteeing agency must make its own evaluation of the project, and the

cost of the loan is raised, as a consequence, by from
one to three percentage points. The two defaults on
IDB ordinary loans to private enterprises in Argentina and Brazil that took place in 1966 have probably
had an influence on subsequent activities of the Bank
out of all proportion to their importance. Particularly in the case of industrial projects, any bank
unable or unwilling to risk failure or default will
have difficulty in promoting enterprise.

A further obstacle for the IDB in making direct
loans is that, as in the case of indirect loans, IDB
resources cannot be used to finance working capital,
buy land, or refinance debts, and the proportion of
the loan that can be used for local expenses is usually limited to a maximum of 25 per cent of the investment.

Although the IDB has developed a program of preinvestment studies that has, in many respects, been
successful, the available facilities have not been
used in the industrial sector as fully as they might
have been, partly because of the time taken to process applications and partly because the cost is
generally reimbursable regardless of the results of
the study, so that the borrower bears the entire
risk. Finally, the IDB cannot participate in capital
stock and does not, as a matter of policy, give
guarantees.[14]

In the light of these considerations, an expert
group appointed by the IDB has proposed the establishment of a regional finance corporation to offer
promotional and financial support to Latin American
industry, principally in the private sector. Its
chief functions would be as follows:

(1) The promotion of enterprises, partic-
     ularly for integration projects and
     export-oriented ventures, making spe-
     cial provision for the marketing and
     distribution of manufactures;

(2) Participation in investments in capi-
     tal stock and in loans for medium-term

working capital, the purchase of capital goods of national origin, and local expenses and investments of industrial projects;[15] and guarantee of the obligations of third persons;

(3)   The furnishing of technical advisory services for the transfer of technology;

(4)   Collaboration in the creation of new instruments for tapping national savings and channeling them into industry;

(5)   The promotion and financing of nontraditional exports.[16]

The experts agreed that "the institution should not be organized primarily to channel external resources but to offer the selective specialized support, both financial and promotional, considered most necessary to Latin American enterprise."[17] Participation would be sought outside, as well as inside, the region, but it was agreed that there should be a Latin American majority in the subscribed capital of the corporation.

The idea of creating a regional finance corporation for Latin America has encountered opposition similar to that faced by the supporters of a regional development bank in the 1950s. It is contended, for example, that the proposed corporation would merely duplicate the work of the IFC. The question, as in the 1950s, relates to the degree of specialization envisaged. A regional finance corporation would specialize in the problems of particular countries and respond to local requirements to an extent not feasible for an agency with worldwide responsibilities.

The IFC is compelled, for practical reasons, to maintain a minimum investment per project in the $1-2 million range, and this in itself limits the scope of its operations. At the same time, the IFC has a policy of not replacing private capital from other sources, which has thus far led, in practice, to a reluctance to participate in the promotion of

new projects. It is envisaged that the new regional
finance corporation, if established, would have
greater flexibility in these and other respects than
does the IFC.

INFRASTRUCTURE

Although economic infrastructure accounts for a
large and growing proportion of the IDB lending,[18] it
does not call for a great deal of comment, and much
of the comment required has already been made in
Chapter 5, above.

As regards the development of power supplies,
the IDB has concentrated on projects for generating,
transmitting, and distributing electrical energy.
Up to the end of 1970, the IDB had made loans totaling
$577 million for such projects. In almost all cases,
the loans had been made to public authorities--whether
national, provincial, or municipal; private enterprise is disappearing in this field in Latin America.
Most of the projects are designed to supply the growing demands for electricity in urban centers, but,
recently, the IDB has begun financing projects of
rural electrification, particularly for consumer
cooperatives.

Two of the projects financed by the IDB involve
international cooperation. The Acaray project in
Paraguay, in addition to providing requirements in
that country, will supply electricity to the neighboring areas of Argentina (province of Misiones) and
Brazil (state of Paraná). Similarly, the expansion
of the generating capacity in the north of Colombia
has been linked up with the adjoining region in
Venezuela.

In addition to employing its own resources for
power projects, the IDB has mobilized other external
funds, amounting to over $200 million, including sup-
pliers' credits advanced by industrial countries exporting the equipment required. The IDB's program
of financing in this field, which began in 1965, is
designed to add 6.7 million kilowatts to the generating

capacity of Latin America by 1974. Since the total
growth of generating capacity for Latin America as a
whole between 1965 and 1974 is estimated at about
24.5 million kilowatts, the IDB is, in effect, contributing to 27 per cent of the total expansion expected during this period.

IDB activity has been restricted in this, as in
other fields, by the slowness of some countries in
formulating viable projects and by the inadequacy of
complementary local resources. Local resources are
usually supplied out of the profits of the borrowing
enterprises and the contributions of public authorities. The ability of enterprises to contribute to
the financing, however, depends fundamentally on the
level of tariffs charged.

Although the loan agreements require the borrowers to maintain the real level of tariffs, erosion
frequently takes place in the process of inflation,
since prices are not always fully adjusted to the
rise in costs. Some improvement has taken place in
this respect in recent years, largely as a result of
pressure exerted by the multilateral lending institutions. Inflation has also affected the ability of
public authorities to make their contributions, and
this has often tended to slow down the completion of
projects.

In the fields of land and maritime transport,
the IDB has invested over $500 million in the con-
struction of roads, out of a total cost of $1 billion,
and has contributed about one-half of the total cost
of fifteen port projects costing $170 million. While
a large proportion of the lending for road construction has been devoted to major highways--such as the
Pan American Highway and the Trans-Chaco Highway--
particular attention has been paid to the needs of
the rural sector and to the impact that suitably
placed roads could have upon the marketing of agricultural produce. In all, the road-construction projects
that the IDB has helped to finance since 1961 will,
when completed, have required the construction of
over 20,000 miles of roads, corresponding to about
7.5 per cent of the total road construction in Latin
America throughout the period.

The IDB began financing telecommunications in 1966. This is the sector of infrastructure in which Latin America is most backward. Major expansion of telecommunications networks has been undertaken with IDB support in Bolivia, Chile, the State of Bahia in Brazil, and the Central American region. Another major activity has been the planning of an inter-American network of telecommunications, linking all the countries of the continent; this is likely to lead, in due course, to the drawing up of major investment projects, offering scope for substantial external financing.

As regards agricultural infrastructure, the IDB has granted loans in the amount of $350 million for the execution of irrigation projects. Although six countries have borrowed for this purpose, Mexico alone accounts for three-quarters of the total amount lent. Considerable difficulties have been experienced in relation to irrigation projects on account of the scarcity of basic information, inadequate understanding of the contribution that irrigation can make to agricultural development, institutional weakness and lack of coordination between the various agencies participating in the study and execution of projects, and deficiencies in water legislation. The IDB has sought to overcome these difficulties by providing technical assistance and commissioning studies where necessary.

SOCIAL DEVELOPMENT

Reference has already been made to the importance attached to the financing of social development in the discussions leading up to the establishment of the IDB and the Alliance for Progress. In October, 1960, the Council of the OAS approved a document entitled the Act of Bogotá, which outlined a broad program of joint effort to improve living standards and social conditions and thereby gave concrete expression to the concept of Operation Pan America originally proposed by President Juscelino Kubitschek of Brazil.[19]

The new approach was based on the belief that the kinds of economic development programs hitherto carried out were bound to be slow in affecting social welfare and that more direct measures were therefore needed to combat poverty, disease, illiteracy, inadequate housing, and malnutrition. The Act of Bogotá called for a review of land-tenure legislation, for a wider and more equitable distribution of landownership, for adequate provision of agricultural credit institutions, and for tax systems and fiscal policies that would assure equitable taxation and encourage the use of idle privately owned land.

Proposals were made for land reclamation and settlement, for increasing the productivity of land already in use, for the construction of farm-to-market and access roads, and for government service programs to help the small farmer. Encouragement was to be given to low-cost housing, to aided self-help housing, to the acquisition and subdivision of land for low-cost housing development, and for industrial housing projects. Educational systems were to be re-examined, with particular attention to mass methods for ending illiteracy and to the training of people for particular tasks in the various economic and social fields.

There was to be expansion of national and local health services, development of health-insurance systems, eradication of malaria and other communicable diseases, provision of drinking water, and the introduction of nutrition programs for low-income groups. Noting that such a program required the mobilization of domestic resources, the Act of Bogotá called for an examination of tax schedules, assessment practices, and collection procedures. It suggested that a fair share of additional revenue should be allocated to social development programs. At the same time, in Chapter II of the Act, the Latin American delegations welcomed the decision of the U.S. Government to establish a special inter-American fund for social development, to be administered by the IDB.

Nine years later, in 1970, social projects accounted for only 11 per cent of total IDB lending,

compared with 46 per cent in 1961, and the functions
of the special fund for social development--the SPTF
--had long since been transferred to the FSO. Unlike
the case of industrial lending, the decline in IDB
activity in the field of social projects was not offset by other agencies.[20]

Within the total of social development lending,
however, support for education has increased, while
the declines have taken place in water supply and
sewage systems and in urban development and housing.
(The reasons for these declines have already been
referred to in Chapter 5, above.) In the educational
field, the IDB helps to finance technical and voca-
tional training and has devoted particular attention
to building up the sciences. The composition of its
lending for education from 1961 to 1969 (amounting
to $137.6 million in all) was as follows (in per
cent):

Engineering	24.6
Natural sciences	21.4
Agricultural sciences	13.1
Health sciences	4.1
Social sciences	.9
General education	.6
Technical and vocational training	13.9
Institutional development	21.4
	100.0

IDB funds are, for the most part, spent on the construction of buildings, equipment for teaching and
research, bibliographical material, the training of
instructors, and technical assistance. The Bank
looks with particular favor on projects that include
provision for scholarships and other assistance to
low-income students.

TECHNICAL ASSISTANCE AND
PREINVESTMENT ACTIVITIES

Under its Charter, the IDB is required to provide technical assistance "for the preparation, financing, and implementation of development plans and
projects, including the study of priorities and the
formulation of specific project proposals."[21] Subsequently, the agreement establishing the SPTF required the IDB to provide technical assistance for
the mobilization of the financial resources of member
countries and the strengthening of their financial
institutions.

The IDB has interpreted these provisions as requiring it to furnish the finances needed by member
countries to obtain the services of technical consultants, but not necessarily to provide these services itself directly, except in the field of training. The IDB has taken the view that, in most cases,
the recipient institutions can decide for themselves
what consultants they need, subject to its approval
only where IDB financing is requested. Thus, the IDB
intervenes in the selection of consultants only when
it is specifically requested to do so.

Side by side with the three-year investment
strategy discussed in Chapter 2, above, the IDB prepares a corresponding program of technical assistance
designed to provide the technical services needed
for formulating, executing, and administering the
projects required. It also takes steps to establish
any programs of training that may be needed.

The financing of technical-assistance programs
may take the form of reimbursable, nonreimbursable,
or conditionally reimbursable loans. Up to the end
of 1970, $151.8 million had been committed for tech-
nical assistance, of which $117.8 million consisted
of reimbursable loans, with the remainder provided
on a grant basis. Even where technical-assistance
loans are reimbursable, the IDB prefers to use soft
resources from the FSO; only exceptionally are the
ordinary resources of the IDB employed for this
purpose.

The terms for technical-assistance loans include maturities generally varying between five and ten years, with an interest rate of 3 or 4 per cent a year, depending on whether the assistance is in the social or economic field, respectively. Nonreimbursable resources, which are obtained from the net income of the FSO or the SPTF, are used mainly in financing technical assistance for the developing countries of the region.

In general, the technical-assistance program of the IDB falls into three main categories. The first category consists of technical assistance that is tied to specific projects. These include preinvestment activities, discussed more fully below, and assistance in the execution of projects, including the creation or strengthening of any institutions that may be required in the process. The second category of technical assistance consists of training projects, and the third, of special studies and promotional activities.

Finally, the IDB has joined with the UNDP in financing ILPES, in Santiago, which provides training courses in development, assists governments in establishing effective planning machinery and in preparing development programs, and carries out studies required to improve planning techniques in Latin America.

PREINVESTMENT

The IDB places particular emphasis on the need for assistance to Latin American countries in preinvestment activities. Preinvestment may be broadly defined as the complex of activities designed to identify investment opportunities, select those of greatest importance to the economy, and prepare projects accordingly. It also includes efforts to strengthen and improve the institutional machinery for executing projects.

If there is to be a steady program of mutually supporting investment projects in a country, an essential prerequisite is that a corresponding flow of continuous preinvestment activity be planned and

maintained. This necessitates a scale of operations
and a volume of financial and technical resources
that, in developing countries, are usually to be
found only in the public sector.

Private firms are usually too small to engage
in a continuous exploration of investment opportunities or even to contract for such exploration from
outside consultants. Even large firms in Latin America make relatively little use of contracted technical services. Particularly in the case of industry,
preinvestment studies are generally provided by the
suppliers of equipment or by consultant firms associated with such suppliers.

The difficulty with outside consultants is that
they bring with them a predisposition to recommend
the use of products manufactured by the North American or European companies with which they are associated or of which they have experience. They are
often unfamiliar with the possibilities of using
locally produced machinery or of adapting equipment
to local needs. Moreover, the tendency of outside
consultants to rely on foreign-made machinery may
have profound indirect, as well as direct, effects
on import requirements insofar as such machinery itself often necessitates the importation of intermediate products and components because of very rigorous
specifications that preclude the use of locally fab-
ricated equivalents. There is thus an intimate relationship between the importation of engineering
consultants from abroad and dependence on external
sources of supply for equipment, intermediate products, and construction materials.

The result is that projects undertaken with
foreign assistance tend to have a considerably higher
import content than they need to have in light of
local resources and productive facilities. Since
most developing countries suffer from severe pressure
on their balances of payments, projects designed with
excessively high import requirements may have seriously adverse effects on the long-run growth potential of the countries concerned. By the same token,
new projects do not give as much stimulus to the

economy as they should, since they are not planned
in a manner that would make the utmost use of local
resources and local industrial capacities or that
would encourage the growth of domestic capital-goods
industries.

The IDB therefore considers one of its most important tasks to be the fostering and strengthening
of Latin American consulting enterprises. It is not
suggested that foreign consultants not be used at
all--quite the contrary. A need is seen for local
firms to join together with foreign consultants so
that projects are designed in a manner that would
ensure the transfer of appropriate technologies,
while using locally produced goods, wherever this
can be done in a manner that is consistent with the
success of the project as a whole.

One of the greatest difficulties facing Latin
American consulting firms results from the fluctua-
tions in investment activity characteristic of developing countries, which inevitably leads to fluc-
tuating demand for the services of consultants.
Another problem is that Latin American consultants
are rarely able to compete with their counterparts
from the developed countries in offering ancillary
services and in facilitating access to resources for
financing not merely the preinvestment studies themselves but the subsequent investment projects as
well.

The IDB therefore cooperates with members in
establishing National Preinvestment Funds, which
should be in a position to encourage and stimulate
the growth of local firms of consulting engineers
capable of providing much or most of the preinvestment analysis that is needed in the region. Most of
these funds are still in their early stages. Two
basic types of operation are envisaged for them:
studies of investment opportunities and prefeasibility
and studies of feasibility and engineering requirements. (Prefeasibility studies provide a preliminary
analysis of investment opportunities with a view to
determining whether more extensive and more costly
studies are called for.) The first group of studies

are essentially of a promotional nature and are
therefore predominantly a government responsibility.
The second group of studies are directly related to
investment and may therefore be undertaken both in
the public and in the private sector.

The IDB considers that governments should have
the utmost freedom of action in exploring possible
investment opportunities. This means that they ought
to put up the bulk of the resources for such studies
themselves and that whatever external resources are
obtained should not have any strings attached to
them. In July, 1966, the IDB established the Preinvestment Fund for Latin American Integration. This
fund has similar objectives at the regional level to
those of the National Preinvestment Funds at the country level. Its main areas of activity are described
in Chapter 8, below.

The IDB is aware that not all Latin American
countries are in a position to develop all the preinvestment services that they require, at any rate
in the near future. Thus, there is a need to assist
in financing the export of consultant services from
one Latin American country to another on competitive
terms--in a manner analogous to the scheme for financing intraregional exports of capital goods.

NOTES

1. Australia, Canada, and Denmark all derive
less than 10 per cent of their gross domestic product
from agriculture.

2. It should be noted, however, that, although
the IDB loans shown in Table 18 include both foreign-
and local-currency components, World Bank lending is
entirely in the form of foreign exchange.

3. See Rubens Vaz da Costa, "El BID y La Banca
de Fomento," in Felipe Herrera and others, Década,
p. 255.

4. Ibid., p. 256.

5. U.N., ECLA, Second United Nations Development Decade: Agricultural Development in Latin America (E/CN.12/829), February 12, 1969. (The above data exclude Argentina, where average agricultural incomes are higher and the disparity between upper- and lower-income groups is smaller.)

6. Ibid.

7. ILPES/CELADE, Elementos para la Elaboración de una Politica de Desarrollo con Integración en América Latina (Santiago de Chile: ILPES, 1968), p. 317.

8. ADB press release, No. 26/71, August 31, 1971.

9. A discussion of the policy considerations involved in this view can be found in Chapter 4, above.

10. Based on data for the IDB, IBRD, IDA, AID, and EXIMBANK, but excluding the IFC. IFC financing of Latin American industry from 1961 to 1967 was about one-fifth larger than that of the IBRD.

11. IDB, Analysis.

12. Ibid., p. 68.

13. The World Bank operates in a similar manner.

14. Policy on guarantees is explained in the last section of Chapter 4, above.

15. IDB policy on the financing of local costs is discussed in Chapter 4, above.

16. See Ibid., p. 1.

17. Ibid., p. 3.

18. The proportion was 48.6 per cent in 1968–69, if agriculture is excluded. If the infrastructure component of agriculture is included, the proportion was over 60 per cent at that time.

19. The Act of Bogotá had been drawn up by the so-called Committee of Twenty-one of the OAS, which had met in Bogotá in September, 1960. The Act is contained in the <u>Final Report of the Secretary-General of the Organization of American States on the Third Meeting of the Special Committee to Study the Formulation of New Measures for Economic Cooperation</u>, OEA/Ser. G/IV/C-i-487, Rev. 2 (Washington, D.C., 1960).

20. The combined share of education, housing, and water supply and sewage systems in the total lending of the IDB, IBRD, IDA, AID, and EXIMBANK declined from 20.2 per cent in 1961 to 10.2 per cent in 1967.

21. IDB, <u>Agreement</u>, Art. I, sec. 2 (a)(v).

7

**PROJECTS,
PROGRAMS,
AND
PERFORMANCE**

THE MANDATE

The IDB Charter provides that "loans made or guaranteed by the Bank shall be principally for financing projects, including those forming part of a national or regional development program."[1] This provision of the IDB Charter corresponds to a similar requirement in the Articles of Agreement of the World Bank to the effect that, except in special circumstances, the World Bank's lending shall be directed to specific projects.

The first question that arises is: What is a specific project? According to one definition,

> A project is any unit of expenditure, which, for reasons of administration, accounting, or purpose, it is convenient to define as such. It may range from a grand river-valley scheme to a school, or a small team of experts. A "program" is used in the sense of a set of projects which are linked together in that they are economically so complementary that if one is to be carried out then all should be; or that they are all intended to be carried out in a certain period by the same administrative unit.[2]

And the World Bank points out that

> many different sorts of undertakings are,
> for the purposes of Bank lending, consid-
> ered to be projects. In effect, the only
> requirement imposed by the specific project
> provision of the Articles is that, before
> a loan is made, there shall be a clear
> agreement both on how the proceeds of the
> loan are to be expended and on what the
> loan is expected to accomplish.[3]

On this interpretation, both the World Bank and the
IDB would have considerable flexibility in their
lending objectives so long as a clear agreement was
reached on the character of the expenditure to be
undertaken. The World Bank goes on to argue, however,
that, if it provided finance for unspecified purposes
or for "vague development programs which have not
been worked out in terms of the projects by which the
objectives of the program were to be achieved," there
would be a danger that the resources made available
would make little or no contribution to the expansion
of productive capacity or output.[4]

Thus, the World Bank and the IDB have deliber-
ately chosen to adopt a restricted definition of the
term "project." For example, it would be perfectly
possible for a lending agency and a borrower to agree
on the financing of particular commodity imports--
such as raw materials and components--to be used in
stepping up the production of certain types of goods
from existing idle capacity. This would appear to
fall within the World Bank's interpretation cited
above, to the effect that there must be clear agreement on how the loan is to be spent and what it is
expected to accomplish. But it would not normally be
regarded by the World Bank or the IDB as a project,[5]
whereas a scheme for enlarging the factory capacity
to produce identically the same goods would rank as
a project. Generally speaking, the typical project
consists of a separately identifiable undertaking
involving substantial capital expenditure, such as
would be required for the construction of some kind
of electric power facility, communications system,
irrigation complex, or productive enterprise.

There are several reasons for this clear preference of the two agencies for project lending, narrowly
defined. A former director of the Economics Department of the World Bank has explained the point as
follows:

> Defaults on international loans were wide-
> spread in the 1930s, and it was concluded
> that a principal reason for the defaults
> was improper use of the funds by the bor-
> rowers. Consequently, when the World Bank
> Charter was being written, a provision
> that Bank lending should be for projects
> was included. Essentially, this meant
> that the Bank should lend only for clearly
> defined and agreed purposes which would
> result in an increase in the productive
> capacity of the borrowing country, and that
> appropriate institutional arrangements in
> that country should exist or should be
> created to ensure that the purposes of the
> loan would be achieved.[6]

PROJECT AND NONPROJECT LENDING

Thus, the main advantage of the project approach
was seen to lie in the fact that it could be readily
ascertained whether the borrowed funds were being
used efficiently and for the purposes intended. But
the approach had other features to recommend it.
For one thing, well-recognized techniques exist for
project appraisal, and it is possible to apply standard requirements regarding feasibility studies,
engineering blueprints, management, financial accounting, and provision of local counterpart resources.

At the same time, to use a favorite expression
of aid officials, project lending provides the opportunity for "institution-building" in the developing
countries--that is, the establishment or strengthening
of institutions capable of planning, appraising, and
executing projects; training skilled and unskilled
personnel; and evaluating project implementation.

The lending agency can also take steps to keep a check on the execution of the projects that it is financing, including the efficiency of management, technical and financial supervision, and, in general, compliance with the terms of the loan agreement. Finally, there are psychological advantages in being able to identify a specific project as representing the contribution of a particular agency to a country's development; the assistance thus given appears more visible than it would if it were supplied in the form of general support for a development program or for the balance of payments.

Notwithstanding the foregoing considerations, there are considerable drawbacks in the concentration of the multilateral lending agencies on project financing. Indeed, the idea that a lending agency has greater assurance that its resources will not be wasted if they are used for project lending rather than for, say, general balance-of-payments support may be based at least in part upon an illusion. Like other lending agencies, the IDB requires that any project it finances should have a high priority within the over-all development program of the recipient country concerned. But the higher the priority assigned to a particular project, the more likely is it that that project would have been undertaken, even in the absence of foreign assistance, and paid for out of earned foreign exchange.

In such a case, the foreign exchange provided by the lending agency, in effect, releases corresponding resources that would otherwise have had to be allocated to the project in question, and these latter resources can then be used to finance other imports at the entire discretion of the borrowing country. Thus, the fact that the lending agency satisfies itself that a particular project is sound and of high priority does not mean that the foreign-exchange resources lent in consideration of that project will not be wasted; for the financing of the project may simply make it possible for the country concerned to increase its imports of, say, luxury consumer goods to an equivalent extent.

If, of course, the lending agency does not pick
its project from the priority list, the project becomes an additional one, and foreign exchange is then
not released for other, possible wasteful, purposes.
But, in that case, other problems arise. In the first
place, it is questionable whether an outside agency
ought to impose its own priorities on a country.
(This point is discussed further, below.) But, to
the extent that it does so, it may add to the strain
on domestic resources, especially since current doc-
trine prevents the lending agencies from financing
more than a small proportion of local costs.

The government may then be faced not merely with
an aggravation of domestic inflationary pressures
but, also, with an enlarged balance-of-payments defi-
cit, due to the spilling over of domestic demand into
imports. In such a case, what started out as an effort by the lending agency to assist in the financing
of imports essential for development ends up as an
additional strain on the foreign-exchange resources
of the country concerned.

The basic difficulty with project financing is
its rigidity--that is, its limited adaptability to
the specific situations of individual countries.
There are two characteristic features of an ideal
project for multilateral financing under existing
conditions. The first is that it should be on a sufficiently large scale--the average IDB project involves a loan of $11-12 million and a total outlay,
including the local contribution, of at least $20
million. The second is that the imported component
of total expenditure should be relatively high, because of restrictions on the financing of local costs.

But, in many countries, the inventory of projects
possessing the above features may be too small to
yield the total volume of assistance needed in light
of their over-all development programs and trade
prospects. And, even if a sufficient number of projects that would be suitable for international financing can be worked up, these may be of lower priority
for the economy than are other types of expenditure.

For example, there are circumstances in which imports of raw materials, components, and spare parts for existing industry may be much more important for the health of an economy than is investment in new large-scale projects. Such a situation could arise in a country with a significant manufacturing capacity of its own that was unable to utilize that capacity fully because of a shortage of foreign exchange to finance imported inputs.

The provision of additional massive projects for such a country may be considerably less helpful to it than enabling it to use part of the available foreign exchange to purchase the imports required for increasing the rate of utilization of existing capacity. If part of the external resources were made available in the form of nonproject, instead of project, aid under such conditions, this would permit the country to raise its level of production and income, thereby generating additional local savings that could be used to finance the domestic costs of any new projects.

By the same token, a potentially serious consequence of the tying of assistance to new projects, combined with local financing of domestic costs, is that the recipient country is given an incentive to choose projects with as high an import content as possible, even though this may mean leaving domestic productive capacity idle. This illustrates the dangers in the concentration of multilateral lending on large-scale infrastructure projects, to the detriment of more direct support and stimulus to productive activity in smaller projects that would make better use of local capacity and skills. There is also a danger of biasing investment in favor of capital-intensive projects that would not necessarily be the ones chosen if the aid resources were made available in the form of freely disposable foreign exchange. Thus, import and investment patterns tend to become distorted by the inflexibility of aid-financed projects.

Project-tied loans are also very slow in being disbursed. To the extent that this is due to the

requisite building up of the recipient country's
capacity to operate the project effectively, nothing
is lost thereby. But much of the delay results from
the complexities of the operations of the multilateral
agencies themselves. The consequences of this in the
case of industrial programs were discussed in Chapter
6, above.

Finally, project lending is much less amenable
than nonproject lending to short-run adjustments.
The pipeline of project lending is a relatively long
one, measured in years rather than months, and the
momentum of disbursements at any particular time
therefore depends on decisions taken a long time be-
forehand. This is not necessarily a disadvantage
from a long-run standpoint, since steadiness and con-
tinuity in the flow of resources are most desirable
for effective development planning. Nevertheless,
experience shows a constant need to adjust long- and
medium-term plans in the light of current conditions,
and there is a corresponding need to be able to vary
the level of assistance provided, within reasonable
limits.

An important instance in which such flexibility
is needed is the case where a country encounters an
unexpected drop in export receipts for reasons beyond
its control--as a result, say, of a poor harvest or
a sudden decline in external demand, whether for
cyclical or secular reasons. This is the situation
for which the United Nations Conference on Trade and
Development's (UNCTAD) proposal for supplementary
financing was designed. The proposal was intended
to make it possible for IDA to provide nonproject
assistance in the circumstances indicated above--
something that IDA would not otherwise be permitted
to do. There is no reason why such a scheme could
not be operated by the regional development banks if
there were the necessary support from the developed
countries for allowing the multilateral institutions
to engage in nonproject lending. Thus far, however,
proposals of this type have attracted only limited
support among the developed countries.

The Pearson Commission expressed the view that
"current aid funds would be more effectively used if

a larger share were supplied in the more flexible
form of program aid." It also recommended that IDA
should "undertake program lending wherever appropriate,
seeking, if necessary, statutory change to make this
possible." The Commission coupled this with a recommendation for greater help to development banks and
similar institutions in developing countries.[7]

Nonproject loans are not a new device to bilateral lenders. In fact, of the total bilateral commitments of financial resources in 1967 (excluding
technical assistance), no less than 58 per cent was
in the form of nonproject loans. The contrast with
the IDB and the World Bank is therefore a vivid one.
Any tendency to channel a larger proportion of the
total flow of resources through the multilateral
agencies--which may, on other grounds, be desirable--
would, as matters stand, introduce greater rigidity
into the system unless the multilateral institutions
were authorized to go in for nonproject lending.

NONPROJECT LENDING
AND LEVERAGE

It is of interest to consider why nonproject
lending forms such a high proportion of bilateral
assistance and such a small proportion of multilateral
flows. The main reason is probably that there is a
larger political element in the aid programs of the
bilateral donors and a more direct link to broad considerations relating to the "performance" and policies
of the recipient countries.

A good deal of thought has been devoted to the
use of aid to influence the policies of recipient
countries.[8] In a paper published by AID in 1966,
Joan M. Nelson and Gustav Ranis, who were officials
of AID at the time, expressed the view that the "influence potential" of aid is more important than is
its resource contribution. Two reasons were given
for this. In the first place, aid from all sources
provides only about 20 per cent of the total investment of developing countries, and the use made of
the remaining 80 per cent is therefore much more

important in accelerating growth than is the aid contribution alone. In the second place, the policies
employed in seeking to accelerate development are at
least as important as is the additional capital financed by aid.[9]

Nelson and Ranis go on to distinguish between
the more general concept of influence and the narrower
concept of leverage, as follows:

Leverage goes beyond influence and persua-
sion to condition aid, explicitly or implic-
itly, on specified host country action.
Leverage may be negative or positive: aid
may be withheld unless certain conditions
are satisfied, or additional aid may be made
available if host country performance
achieves specified standards. Positive leverage is sometimes called "incentive pro-
gramming."[10]

Project lending can be, and often is, used to
exert both general influence and specific leverage
on actions by recipient countries. Various requirements are imposed by lending agencies on borrowing
governments and enterprises, such as meeting engineering and technical criteria, contributing to local
costs, and establishing adequate machinery for operating and maintaining projects; and, in a broader
sense, adequate efforts to achieve monetary stability
may also be required of recipient countries. Thus,
the lending agencies, both bilateral and multilateral,
consider it important to make use of their assistance
programs for insisting on what they regard as "good
performance."

As the director of the Western Hemisphere Department of the World Bank, Gerald M. Alter, has put it,
borrowing countries

must feel that the carrot of sizeable loans
can be withdrawn with drastic consequences
to their economic development. . . . The
credibility of aid is ultimately linked to
its volume and quantity. No developing

country will take the recommendations of the
Bank seriously if it feels that the Bank is
not prepared to follow through on its loans.
The quantity of aid therefore has a psychological impact on developing countries and
their attitudes towards the Bank.[11]

Nevertheless, nonproject lending has been found
more effective for influencing economic policies than
has project lending.[12]   Large-scale investment projects of the type characteristically financed by the
multilateral institutions, including the IDB, take
many years to plan, design, negotiate, execute, and
bring to completion. Such projects, once started,
acquire a life and a tempo of their own and are
therefore not well suited to the kind of short-term
variations in the volume of assistance that may be
required if material incentives are to be provided
to recipient countries to effect changes in their
policies in the sense desired by the lenders.

Nonproject loan agreements between AID and Brazil,
Chile, and Colombia provided that assistance would be
released in quarterly tranches contingent on host-
country performance, as measured by agreed indicators;
and an agreement with the Republic of Korea provided
"incentive funds" for five specific policy reforms--
progress on any one of them would be "rewarded" with
a small increment in the total program loan, and adequate performance on all five would result in the
release of the full $10 million provided under the
loan agreement.[13]

Some observers, however, are uneasy about some
of the implications of leverage--particularly where
it is used for the achievement of political objectives
--and would therefore prefer to see the multilateral
agencies stay clear of nonproject lending. Thus,
for example, Orlando Letelier, former director in
the IDB Operations Department, writes as follows:

We believe that there are many factors in-
dicating that the IDB should maintain its
present orientation of using its resources
for proposals that lead to clearly defined

projects or programs. . . . It is unrealistic to suppose that a multilateral development bank, using measuring instruments that
do not exist and operating in an ideal world
which does not exist either, could provide
finance for the general requirements of a
particular country on the basis of norms
purporting to reflect an evaluation in precise terms of the development effort of a
country. . . . The fact of operating within
the framework of specific projects and programs clearly does not obviate the necessity of having proposals submitted to the
Bank examined from a macroeconomic point of
view as well. . . . The Bank should benefit from the general orientation . . . given
by the Inter-American Committee for the Alliance for Progress (CIAP) on the basis of
its periodic examinations of progress in
the various Latin American countries.[14]

In order to understand the relationship of CIAP appraisals to the operations of the IDB, it is necessary to review the origins of these appraisals.

CIAP APPRAISALS

The Alliance for Progress had defined the goal
of cooperative efforts in the western hemisphere in
terms of a broad acceleration of economic and social
progress, combined with a wider distribution of the
benefits of such progress. Specific instruments
were envisaged for this purpose--reform of agrarian
structures, modernization of tax policies, improved
administration of the public sector, and more emphasis on investment in social projects.

The Charter of Punta del Este, adopted in August,
1961, established a panel of nine high-level experts
attached to the Inter-American Economic and Social
Council, but enjoying complete autonomy in the performance of their duties. Each government, if it so
desired, could present its program for economic and
social development for consideration by an ad hoc

committee composed of not more than three members of
the panel of nine.

The committee was to study the development program, exchange views with the government concerned
about possible modifications, and, then, with the
consent of the government, report its conclusions to
the IDB and to governments and institutions that might
be prepared to provide assistance in support of the
program. An important element in the committee's
consideration of a country's program was to be its
consistency with the Charter of Punta del Este and
with the Act of Bogotá[15]--that is, with the economic
and social goals referred to above.[16]

The IDB was to assist governments in obtaining
the external resources required for the implementation of their programs, notably from AID, EXIMBANK,
the World Bank, and, of course, the IDB itself. This
was laid down in the Charter of Punta del Este in
the following terms:

> A government whose development program has
> been the object of recommendations made by
> the ad hoc committee with respect to ex-
> ternal financing requirements may submit
> the program to the Inter-American Develop-
> ment Bank so that the Bank may undertake
> the negotiations required to obtain such
> financing, including the organization of
> a consortium of credit institutions and
> governments disposed to contribute to the
> continuing systematic financing, on appro-
> priate terms, of the development program.[17]

The approach of Punta del Este was subsequently
modified in two respects. First, the IDB did not,
in practice, assume the central role in negotiating
for assistance for each country, as had been proposed.
Second, it was decided, in 1963, to establish a multilateral forum--known as the Inter-American Committee
for the Alliance for Progress (CIAP)--to promote aid
coordination and self-help. CIAP has a full-time
chairman and seven members selected on the same basis
as the Executive Directors of the IDB. Ex officio

members include the President of the IDB, the Executive Secretary of ECLA, and the Secretary-General of the OAS.

CIAP operates on two levels. On the one hand, CIAP members meet to consider and make recommendations concerning questions of regional policy. On the other hand, CIAP organizes an annual series of country reviews, each review being attended by the external financial agencies (including the IDB, IMF, World Bank, and AID) and representatives of the member country concerned. In 1966, the U.S. Congress sought to strengthen the force of CIAP recommendations concerning individual countries, based on the annual reviews, by introducing a clause into the Foreign Assistance Act requiring U.S. assistance to be consistent with these recommendations.

In light of the annual reviews, countries expecting to receive external assistance voluntarily undertake commitments to adopt certain policies and measures. These commitments are specified in a letter of intent addressed by the governments concerned to CIAP. They include, typically, commitments regarding the steps to be taken to increase agricultural and industrial production, to promote investment in certain key sectors, to encourage various types of exports, to reduce the rate of inflation, to expand tax revenues, to maintain a realistic exchange rate, and so forth.[18]

In connection with the enlargement of IDB resources in 1967, the Bank decided to strengthen its cooperation with CIAP and the other lending agencies, including AID, through the appointment of a Program Adviser at the head of a small planning staff in the office of the President of the IDB. By this means, the Bank undertook, when programing the use of its resources, including those of the expanded FSO, to take account of the development efforts of its members, as assessed by CIAP. While the Bank remained responsible for its own decisions, it accepted the consensus on each country's performance reached jointly in CIAP as a significant factor in the allocation of financial resources to members. The IDB

also looked to CIAP as a forum in which the lending
programs of the various agencies could be coordinated
with one another and with the goals of the Latin American countries.

In their April, 1970, report dealing with the
need for an increase in the resources of the IDB, the
Board of Executive Directors of the IDB defined the
relationship between the Bank's lending policies and
the performance of member countries in the following
terms:

> The Bank over the past three years has lent
> its support fully to CIAP efforts to bring
> about improvements in performance which
> country reviews have revealed to be defi-
> cient and an impediment to the sound execu-
> tion of development programs. The record
> of Bank action indicates that lending neces-
> sarily tends to fall off in those countries
> with severe performance problems, whose ca-
> pability to absorb and use development re-
> sources has been markedly reduced through
> inadequate fiscal, monetary and administra-
> tive policies. At the same time, the Bank
> has held to the view that in some circum-
> stances countries having internal problems
> may be benefited by continued assistance
> through technical advice and, in certain
> situations, continued lending though at a
> reduced level and only for programs with
> minimal budgetary impact until the obsta-
> cles which impede progress have been re-
> duced or eliminated.
>
> The Bank will continue its attention to in-
> ternal problems as an important element af-
> fecting development and will support the
> multilateral efforts of CIAP, in coopera-
> tion with other international and bilat-
> eral lenders, to encourage the adoption,
> where deemed necessary, of the policy mea-
> sures and structural changes that would
> enable each nation to achieve more effec-
> tive and enduring progress toward economic
> development and social improvement.[19]

This being the case, it hardly seems that there is any difference, in principle, between the use of project lending and nonproject lending for influencing performance. The most that can be said is that nonproject lending may be much more effective where the intention is to bring strong pressure to bear on recipient countries. But those who object to such pressure can scarcely maintain that it is a feature only of nonproject lending. Both forms of lending can be undertaken with or without the intent to exert influence on the recipient country, depending on the wishes of the lending agency concerned. Thus, the advantages of nonproject lending may be assessed independently of its relationship to performance.

THE MEANING OF GOOD PERFORMANCE

Although the IDB has thus indicated its full support for "CIAP efforts to bring about improvements in performance" and has even warned that lending "tends to fall off" where there are severe performance problems, it is far from clear what is to be understood by "good performance" in a country. It is particularly uncertain how much remains of the strict injunctions of the Charter of Punta del Este and of the Act of Bogotá regarding the measures of reform, structural change, and social justice considered, in 1961, to be indispensable for progress by all participating governments.

Thus, the Charter of Punta del Este, which initiated the Alliance for Progress, stated as its first objective of policy its determination to "improve and strengthen democratic institutions through application of the principle of self-determination by the people." It then went on to advocate "programs of comprehensive agrarian reform, leading to the effective transformation, where required, of unjust structures and systems of land tenure and use" and the replacement of "latifundia and dwarf holdings by an equitable system of property."

It also called for tax reform, "demanding more from those who have most," and undertaking "to punish tax evasion severely." On social objectives the

Charter of Punta del Este proclaimed the need for wiping out illiteracy and enlarging educational facilities, pressing forward with programs of health and sanitation, carrying out urban and rural housing programs, and improving the distribution of income.

The question arises whether the rate of progress toward (or away from) these goals should form part of an assessment of a country's performance. If it does, it is impossible to escape the need for all kinds of political and social value judgments. If it does not, there may be many cases in which it could be shown that a country had achieved a high rate of growth of output, a rising proportion of income saved, and a high degree of monetary stability while, at the same time, moving backward in terms of social equity and political freedom. Where would such a country be ranked on the scale of performance?

In practice, this question has become somewhat academic during the period that has elapsed since the Charter of Punta del Este was adopted. The staff of the Pearson Commission reports that the exhilaration produced by the Charter of Punta del Este has been replaced by skepticism and that disillusion with the Alliance for Progress is widespread, neither side having kept all its commitments. Moreover, "official aid has not always been granted purely on development criteria, nor in amounts or on conditions consistent with achieving the 1961 social and economic goals."[20]

In these circumstances, it is not surprising that there has been a tendency to place greater emphasis on the attainment of fiscal and monetary stability than on the introduction of really serious and far-reaching measures for restructuring the economy, notably through land reform and tax reform. Hirschman and Bird have pointed to "the increasing tendency to make program aid depend on the taking of specific monetary and exchange-rate measures and on the 'appropriate' behavior of certain fiscal and monetary indicators, while less and less attention is paid to economic growth and social justice, supposedly the principal objectives of aid."[21] Thus, although measures to improve fiscal and monetary

stability have often been made a condition of assistance, the granting of aid has never been made conditional upon the adoption of effective reform.

This, of course, involves a significant value
judgment. It means that the balancing of the budget,
the curbing of the money supply, and the adoption of
an appropriate exchange rate are still regarded as
more important for the economic health of a country
than is the redistribution or reorganization of the
large underutilized estates or the introduction of
effective and equitable methods of taxation so as to
mobilize resources for development and lessen in-
equalities in income and wealth. The effect (although not necessarily the intention) of the value
judgment thereby adopted may be to give greater importance to maintaining an appropriate economic balance within the existing order of things than to
changing that order.

A further point that deserves some emphasis is
that, as Joan M. Nelson points out, explicit leverage
may achieve its objectives in the narrow sense of
bringing about the changes in exchange rate or other
policies that are sought. But this does not mean
that the chosen policies will necessarily prove to
be effective in restoring balance-of-payments equi-
librium or slowing down inflation.

Several of the developed countries, including
the United States and the United Kingdom, have encountered great difficulties in attaining these very
same goals, and there is no reason why these problems
should be easier to solve in the developing coun-
tries--quite the contrary. Thus, the international
agencies run the risk not merely of incurring serious
criticism by seeking to impose policies on unwilling
governments but, also, of finding the criticism compounded by the failure of the policies imposed.

THE MEASUREMENT OF PERFORMANCE

A basic difficulty in applying performance criteria to the distribution of aid is that, although

much thought and research have been devoted to the
problem of measuring the development effort of countries, it cannot be said that this work has yielded
generally accepted standards of effort. In a recent
study, the UNCTAD Secretariat pointed out that:

> The attempt to identify reasonable "standards
> of effort" at once raises the question how
> to use the available indicators to distin-
> guish "effort" from "success." One country
> may succeed virtually without effort, be-
> cause of some windfall such as the discov-
> ery of rich oil resources. Another may
> fail notwithstanding intense effort, because
> of unfavourable circumstances beyond its
> control. The problem is to find quantita-
> tive indicators that would clearly identify
> what is good fortune in the case of the one
> and misfortune in the case of the other.
>
> The difficulty is that the indicators that
> are usually regarded as providing the best
> measures of "effort" are themselves strongly
> affected by external circumstances beyond
> the control of the countries concerned.
> Thus, in the above example, the country gain-
> ing fortuitous success will simultaneously
> record high and rising savings ratios and
> rapid increases in government revenue from
> taxation while the country afflicted by,
> say, a succession of bad harvests or a col-
> lapse of external demand for its main export
> products will show a poor record as regards
> savings and tax revenue.[22]

For the purposes of its analysis, the UNCTAD
Secretariat ranked some fifty developing countries
in descending order of the ratio of gross domestic
savings to gross domestic product for the period
1950-65. It was found that the distinguishing characteristic of the countries ranking at the top of the
list--namely, Kuwait, Liberia, Venezuela, and Iraq--
was not so much the vigor of their development efforts
as the favorable experience that they had had with

their exports. High and increasing ratios of savings
to income in these and other countries were found to
reflect high and rising shares of business profits
in income, and the latter were, in turn, the result
of high rates of growth of production and exports.
Conversely, countries that were relatively low in
the rankings had had much less favorable experience
with their exports.[23]

Moreover, there was no relationship between rankings of countries in terms of the savings ratio and
in terms of the growth rate: The country with the
lowest savings ratio--Jordan--had the highest total
and per capita rates of growth over the same period.
The Republic of Korea--generally regarded as one of
the success stories among developing countries--
ranked second from the bottom in terms of its average
savings ratio.

It is not, of course, suggested that the savings
ratios are entirely the result of factors outside the
control of the countries concerned. The point is,
rather, that it has proved very difficult, if not impossible, to determine how much of a country's savings
performance is due to its own deliberate efforts and
sacrifice and how much is due entirely to chance factors, such as the trend of market demand for its exports. In these circumstances, it is not possible
to set a standard for savings effort that could be
applied unambiguously.

The Pearson Commission brushed this problem
aside:

> If it were necessary to give each country
> a precise rating for performance, the as-
> sessors would bog down in determing the
> relative weights to be ascribed to differ-
> ent policies. However, such precision is
> not needed. Those who report on perfor-
> mance do not need to award an overall mark;
> and those who allocate funds will have lit-
> tle difficulty in distinguishing between
> good, mediocre and bad performance.[24]

This is an extraordinarily optimistic view, to
say the least. It is indeed easy to distinguish between success and failure or between high and low
rates of growth. But the distinction between good
and bad performance is much more elusive and depends,
moreover, on the level at which the problem is considered. Should performance be evaluated after taking into account the prevailing political, social,
and economic constraints, or without regard to these
constraints?

It might be said that a particular country had
turned in a mediocre performance if viewed against
some absolute and theoretical standards, without reference to the social context; but a quite different
conclusion might be reached if due weight were given
to the political and social obstacles that the country had faced and the way in which it had sought to
deal with them, even though these efforts may have
come to nothing for the time being.

Moreover, the Pearson Commission's idea of leaving it to "those who allocate funds" to make the distinction between good, mediocre, and bad performance
is unlikely to prove generally acceptable. If this
distinction cannot be drawn on the basis of precise
standards, but only by intuition, there are bound to
be honest differences of opinion between equally competent observers.

The important thing is not merely that the allocation of funds should be fair but, also, that it
should be seen to be fair, and this is impossible if
there are no precise standards. Certainly, any incentive effect of distributing aid in proportion to
performance would be largely dissipated if the recipient countries were unable to understand what
criteria and standards were being applied. Thus, a
great deal more empirical analysis of performance
would have to be undertaken before the allocation of
aid could be made to depend on it in any scientific
way.

There is also a considerable danger that, where
evidence of good performance is required as part of

the justification of assistance from a national or
international agency, the criteria applied may differ
from case to case, depending on how large and important the particular developing country may be and on
how firm its opposition to outside interference is.
Small countries may well find themselves much more
vulnerable to outside pressures than are big countries, where more effective opposition can be generated. This can lead to serious inequities in the
treatment of various recipient countries by the lending agencies.

But, even if a number of unambiguous indicators
of good performance could be found and applied even-
handedly to the strong as well as to the weak, would
the international community really want to base itself on such indicators in determining the distribution of aid? This would, in effect, amount to backing efficiency. But a ranking of countries in terms
of their economic efficiency would be quite different
from a ranking in terms of equity--unless one is prepared to argue that only the efficient have a moral
claim to be given assistance.

The latter is certainly not the basis on which
domestic assistance programs are established in the
industrial countries themselves. On the contrary,
welfare programs in the industrial countries often
tend, in effect, to penalize the efficient by limiting their entitlement to assistance. Moreover, industrial assistance, whether in the form of subsidies
or protective tariffs, is often specifically directed
to the weak and the inefficient and may not be available to the efficient at all.

Much of the current concern with efficiency as
a criterion for the distribution of aid is the result
of the over-all inadequacy of the aid effort, which
prompts those dealing with the problem of allocating
aid to try and make the "best use" (in some sense of
that term) of the little that they have. Some observers would also contend that the dispersion of
limited aid resources over a large number of countries
is less effective in the long run than concentrating
first on those with the best prospects of reaching

the point of self-sustaining growth within the foreseeable future.

It is doubtful, however, whether the efficiency
criterion is justified at even the present low level
of assistance. Experience has shown repeatedly that
the lists of good, mediocre, and bad performers
change frequently, with countries moving from one
category to another and back again. It would be extraordinarily difficult to mount a serious long-term
program of aid in any country if it were constantly
necessary to vary the program to suit the latest assessment of performance.

But the real objection to the efficiency criterion is that it is inequitable. And, since the only
valid justification for aid is the moral one, it
would be paradoxical, in the extreme, to determine
the distribution of aid on the basis of an amoral
principle. That is not to say, of course, that one
should not try to encourage the receivers of aid to
make efficient use of their resources, both internal
and external. The argument is not against self-help,
as such, but only against the ranking of countries
in terms of pseudo-scientific self-help criteria as
a means of determining their eligibility for external
assistance.

THE APPLICATION OF
PERFORMANCE CRITERIA

The IDB's policies and practices do not differ
very much from those of other bilateral and multilateral lending agencies in seeking to encourage more-
efficient economic management in its member countries.
Indeed, the IDB regards it as one of its most important contributions to Latin American development to
assist member countries in deriving the maximum benefit from IDB-financed projects, by ensuring that the
projects are planned and implemented in the most effective way possible and that any institutional adjustments that are required are actually undertaken.

The Bank's Charter does, in fact, require it "to
cooperate with the member countries to orient their

development policies toward a better utilization of their resources . . . ."[25] The IDB is therefore active in a variety of fields, including, as noted earlier, the strengthening of planning institutions, the preparation of projects, the establishment or strengthening of institutions capable of executing projects, the training of personnel, and the evaluation and improvement of project implementation.

But aid may be used in seeking to attain objectives much more far-reaching than those outlined above. The crucial question is whether the agency accepts the broad framework of government objectives and policies and seeks only to increase the effectiveness with which they are carried out or whether it goes further to try to influence the fundamental policies and objectives themselves. If it does the latter, it is almost bound to become involved in issues regarded as controversial in the political arena of the country concerned.

What is particularly unfortunate is that policies that may be very sound and well conceived may come to be rejected in a particular country simply because some external agency wishes to impose its will in a particular direction as a condition of lending money. In such cases, national resentment tends to build up to the point at which it ceases to matter whether the policies that are being imposed from outside are reasonable or not. The primary consideration becomes resistance to infringements on national prerogatives, whether the policies advocated are good, bad, or indifferent.

Since most policies for development are also policies for change, it is almost inevitable that a sound development program will generate opposition internally from those quarters that are opposed to change. It may be difficult enough to achieve a mobilization of domestic political forces that will bring about beneficial change even without external pressure, but it can only compound the problem if the forces opposed to change are able to rally to their support the natural instincts of all those who dislike having particular courses of action imposed upon them from abroad as the price of foreign assistance.

For these reasons, it has been a point of some importance with the IDB that the final responsibility for decisions on the formulation of plans, the definition of policies, the establishment of priorities, and the adoption of investment decisions must rest with the member countries and that IDB loans should not be used as a means of exerting pressure in these matters.[26] At the request of a member country, the IDB is prepared to furnish technical assistance on any question of development policy. But, in all such cases, the objective is to support the national decision-making process and not to replace it by the use of outside experts.

The IDB considers that high-level missions from abroad, however competent they may be from a technical standpoint, cannot, in the nature of the case, place themselves in the particular context of each country; and, although the findings of such missions may throw important light on the development problem of a country, their judgments should not be substituted for those of the national authorities, whose responsibility it is to reach an over-all conclusion in light of all factors.

Thus, the IDB, on the one hand, accepts and recognizes the authority of each country in defining its own development objectives and priorities and, on the other hand, verifies that each specific operation undertaken in accordance with these basic national criteria also satisfies the requirements of economic viability, thereby ensuring that the project would make an effective contribution to national development.[27]

In harmony with this approach, a crucial element in IDB policy is the Bank's concern with the development problems of all its Latin American members. As the Manager of the Technical Department of the IDB has put it,

Under other forms of cooperation, agencies or countries providing financial or tech-

nical assistance do not feel called upon
to be present in all areas having development problems. In such cases decisions to
extend assistance have been based chiefly
either on the existence of favorable circumstances, including suitable development
policies, well elaborated projects and effective implementation, or on other considerations of a political or strategic character. Where international assistance
policy is determined in this way, the most
difficult cases, involving countries which
for a variety of reasons encounter major
obstacles to their development, are apt to
be left on one side, unless political or
strategic factors happen to favor them. . . .
From the very beginning of its operations,
the IDB has recognized that one of its
characteristic activities must be to maintain a permanent presence in all its member countries, except where a country explicitly rejects it . . . .[28]

Thus, the IDB did not follow the lead of other
agencies in withholding assistance from Brazil during
the early 1960s; nor did it participate in the denial
of assistance to Colombia at the time that that country was unwilling to accept the recommendations of
the IMF for the stabilization of its economy. This
policy approach appears, however, to have been modified in important respects since 1967, and, as the
statement by the Board of Executive Directors cited
earlier in this chapter pointed out, inadequate fiscal, monetary, and administrative policies in particular countries may lead to a reduction in IDB lending
to such countries.

A more serious problem has arisen as a result
of charges that disagreement on other types of policy,
particularly that involving the treatment of private
foreign investment, may affect the IDB's willingness
to lend to particular countries. In the course of
his inaugural address to the twelfth annual meeting
of the IDB on May 10, 1971, President Juan Velasco
Alvarado of Peru asserted that the international
agencies had followed a policy of discrimination

against Peru because of its program for freeing itself of foreign domination.

Peru had expropriated property of the International Petroleum Company, a subsidiary of Standard
Oil of New Jersey, although the government had also
offered guarantees of fair treatment and "legitimate"
profits to both Peruvian and foreign investors, provided that they were prepared to adjust to the requirements of Peruvian economic and social development
The President of Peru said that the time had come to
make a careful evaluation of the IDB, "which shows
signs of being used as an instrument of political
pressure against countries such as Peru that decide
to break with the past by introducing a policy of
liberation and nationalism that recognizes only the
interests of its people as a standard and goal."[29]
Several other representatives of Latin American countries strongly condemned interference in the internal
affairs of borrowing countries.

In the course of his reply to these criticisms,
the President of the IDB, Antonio Ortiz Mena, said
that distribution of the ordinary resources of the
IDB, on terms related to the Bank's cost of borrowing, was based strictly on an objective evaluation
of projects and on respect for the development plans
and priorities drawn up by the member countries themselves.[30]

The situation was, he said, "quite different"
when the Bank was entrusted with the administration
of special funds, such as the FSO, generally consisting of soft resources. The agreements establishing
these funds enable the country furnishing the whole
or the bulk of the resources to determine the operations to be authorized; no loan could, for example,
be made by the FSO without the approval of the United
States. This, said the President of the IDB, "can
mean the rejection of loans under circumstances or
for reasons that the applicant country considers to
constitute intervention in its internal affairs."

Ortiz Mena suggested that the best safeguard
would be "to diversify the sources of soft funds so

that the borrower country can choose the type of
credit that suits it best. This would create competition among the capital-exporting countries that
would undoubtedly lead to a gradual liberalization of
the conditions imposed on the granting of soft
funds."[31]

PERFORMANCE, LEVERAGE,
AND THE FUTURE

Great concern has been expressed by some of the
most moderate and balanced spokesmen for the developing countries regarding the idea that aid could, or
should be, closely linked to the performance of the
aid receiver. Thus, I. G. Patel has referred to
"the strident style of performance-oriented aid di-
plomacy which smacks of neo-colonialism"; and has
drawn attention

> to instances where the assessment and ad-
> vice of even international agencies have
> been either biased or wrong, thus lending
> support to the thesis that insistence on
> satisfying particular criteria of perfor-
> mance is yet another guise for promoting
> ideological conformity around the world.[32]

It also has been suggested by spokesmen for developing countries that international agencies are
apt to show less judgment in their use of leverage
than are national agencies. Thus, the Minister of
Finance of Malawi told the annual meeting of the IMF
and the World Bank the following on September 21,
1970:

> Because they are often very much more polit-
> ically aware than international institutions
> and international civil servants, bilateral
> donors may often be much more sensitive to
> developing countries' susceptibilities than
> international bodies. Maybe, too, conscious
> as nations are of their own past errors, they
> are less sure that their own views are so
> inevitably superior and correct.

In this connection, it may be noted that international lending agencies are typically staffed with men whose experience lies in technical analysis or the planning and execution of projects, rather than in forming and acting upon political judgments in the light of a whole complex of considerations, both political and technical. It was possibly with these considerations in mind that the Minister of Finance for India, addressing the 1970 annual meeting of the IMF and the World Bank, made the following observation: "Let us also not have any illusions that, in this day and age, any international agency, however well regulated and well staffed, can do anything more than advise and persuade at a general level."

If the foregoing views are at all typical of those now held in the developing countries, it will be apparent that, whether leverage is successful in particular cases or not, neither the national nor the international lending agencies have yet been able to persuade the developing countries of the importance or usefulness of performance norms. On the contrary, there is a certain sharpness about the wording of the statements just cited that suggests sensitivity and resentment on this issue.

One of the most important observations made by the Task Force on International Development appointed by President Nixon (the Peterson Committee) was the following:

> Many developing countries now have the capacity and the experience needed to establish their own development priorities and a strong and understandable determination to do so. They are mobilizing more investment resources themselves, and they have many more well-trained, competent professionals and technicians. The developing countries themselves, therefore, should be at the center of the international development effort. The policies they pursue will be the most important determinant of their success or failure. What the United States and other industrial countries do

will have only a secondary, though essential, influence on the outcome.[33]

Some of the thinking that lies behind the new
approach of the U.S. Government has been described
by Jack Heller, a senior official of AID specializing
in the Latin American region.[34] He begins by stress-
ing the need for humility on the part of those concerned with aid programs, especially since external
assistance can play at best a marginal, although at
times catalytic, role in development.

Heller points out that "development priorities,
programs and projects which are not hammered out on
the budgetary and political anvil of the client country are not likely to be actually carried out." He
considers that there has been--and will continue to
be--growing friction between borrower and lender on
such issues as priority setting, what performance
conditions it is reasonable to attach to a lending
program, the appropriate mix for any project between
domestically furnished and externally furnished resources, and other major policy questions.

Where international lenders press for difficult
or unpopular decisions, they often find themselves
blamed for the internal political consequences.
Heller comments, as follows: "This phenomenon can
be constructive within limits, and the role is one
which external assistance donors should willingly
play. But I doubt whether the U.S. government should
seek to play this role for much longer in the future."

Heller points out that there is now a growing
feeling in many countries that questions of national
priorities and performance are for the developing
countries to determine exclusively for themselves
and that the role of the donors must be limited essentially to that of bankers. Taking this into account, the United States has begun to try to change
the style and methods of its bilateral assistance
program.

Henceforth, the United States will rely far
more heavily on Latin American initiatives

in defining the problems and devising appropriate policies and projects than in the
past. Consistent with this strategy, the
U.S. will stress with its Latin American
partners that the development relationship
is two-sided. Recipient countries clearly
must set, live with, and act upon their own
priorities, without the feeling that there
are overbearing influences intruding in
this process from without. At the same
time international donors, including the
United States government, must reserve
their privilege to refrain from supporting
programs and policies which do not appear,
by international standards, to merit support.

Such standards should be defined within a multilateral
framework, and the question of how to construct such
a framework provides a challenge for the future.

NOTES

1. IDB, Agreement, Art. III, sec. 7 (a)(vi).

2. I. M. D. Little and J. M. Clifford, International Aid (Chicago: Aldine, 1966), p. 188.

3. IBRD, The World Bank, IDA and IFC: Policies
and Operations (Washington, D.C., April, 1968), pp.
43-44.

4. Ibid.

5. Both the World Bank and IDA have made a number of nonproject loans, notably by IDA to India and
Pakistan, and there have been recent indications of
a somewhat more-flexible attitude to such loans.
Nevertheless, the great bulk of lending by the World
Bank Group continues to take the form of project financing.

6. Andrew M. Kamarck, "Appraisal of Country
Economic Performance," in IBRD, Some Aspects of the
Economic Philosophy of the World Bank (Washington,
D.C., September, 1968), p. 9.

7. Partners in Development: Report of the Commission on International Development [Pearson Commission] (New York: Praeger, 1969), pp. 177-79. There is some ambiguity in the term "program lending," since a program may be understood in the sense of a program of specific projects. The Pearson Commission, however, uses the term "program aid" as synonymous with "nonproject aid" and "commodity aid."

8. It has long been recognized that loans on easy terms may give the creditor a special power over the borrower, if he chooses to exercise it. Samuel Johnson made the point neatly, as well as quaintly, when he said that "the way to make sure of power and influence is by lending money confidentially to your neighbors at a small interest, or, perhaps, at no interest at all, and having their bonds in your possession." See James Boswell, Life of Samuel Johnson LL.D. (Chicago: Encyclopaedia Britannica, Inc., 1952), p. 194.

9. Joan M. Nelson and Gustav Ranis, Measures to Ensure the Effective Use of Aid, AID Discussion Paper No. 12 (Washington, D.C., September, 1966), p. 8.

10. Ibid.

11. Society for International Development, International Development, 1968 (New York: Oceana Publications, 1969), p. 248.

12. See Joan M. Nelson, Aid, Influence and Foreign Policy (New York: The Macmillan Co., 1968), p. 75, for a discussion of various ways in which aid was used for political purposes between 1961 and 1966.

13. Nelson and Ranis, Measures to Ensure the Effective Use of Aid, p. 12.

14. See Herrera and others, Década, pp. 50-54.

15. See chapter 6, section entitled "Social Development."

16. Charter of Punta del Este, Title II, Ch. 5.

17. Ibid., par. 7.   See, also, the statement by
C. Douglas Dillon, Under-Secretary of State, to the
Foreign Relations Committee of the U.S. Senate on
June 23, 1959, which included the following passage:
"We feel that this institution [the IDB] will be and
is designed to serve more or less as a clearing house,
that the Latin Americans will presumably take their
projects here in the first instance. And since this
institution is nowhere nearly large enough to handle
their desires, it will be a central organization that
will help them to work out package arrangements
which might involve some financing by this institution
and some by one or two or three of the other institutions, such as the Export-Import Bank and the Development Loan Fund and maybe the World Bank."

18. One such letter, from the government of
Chile, was described in some detail in Raymond F.
Mikesell, The Economics of Foreign Aid (Chicago,
Aldine, 1968), pp. 174-76.

19. IDB, Proposal for an Increase in the Resources of the Inter-American Development Bank (Washington, D.C., April, 1970), par. 3.10.

20. Partners in Development, pp. 244-45.

21. A. O. Hirschman and Richard M. Bird, Foreign
Aid--A Critique and a Proposal (Princeton, N.J.:   In-
ternational Finance Section, Princeton University,
July, 1968), p. 11.

22. U.N., The Measurement of Development Effort
(U.N. Sales No.:   E.71.II.D.4), 1970, pars. 4-5.

23. Ibid., pars. 48-63.

24. Partners in Development, p. 132.

25. IDB, Agreement, Art. I, sec. 2 (a)(iv).

26. Cecilio Morales, in Herrera and others,
Década, pp. 205-7.

27. Ibid., p. 208.

28. Ibid., p. 203.

29. Although the President did not mention the
nature of the pressure to which exception was taken,
a subsequent statement by the Peruvian Minister of
Economy and Finance argued that it had taken five
years to process a loan for $11.8 million for con-
struction of the Jaen-San Ignacio Highway "owing to
reasons that had little to do with the evaluation of
the project. . . . This type of disguised pressure
must be definitively abandoned in the Bank's activities." For the texts of the above statements see
IDB, Documents of the XII Meeting of the Board of
Governors (Lima, May, 1971), Nos. AB-263 and AB-267.

30. For further comment on the degree of independence of the IDB in lending from its ordinary resources, see the last section of Chapter 3, above.

31. Ibid., No. ABD-279.

32. I. G. Patel, "Aid Relationship for the Sev-
enties," in The Widening Gap, ed. by Barbara Ward,
J. D. Runnalls, and Lenore D'Anjou (New York: Colum-
bia University Press, 1971), pp. 300 and 302.   Dr.
Patel, who is Permanent Secretary of the Ministry of
Finance of India, wrote this paper in his personal
capacity.

33. U.S. Foreign Assistance in the 1970's: A
New Approach, Report to the President from the Task
Force on International Development (Washington, D.C.,
March 4, 1970), p. 9.

34. Jack Heller, "Development Assistance Strate-
gies in Latin America," Development Digest, VIII, 3
(July, 1970), 118-21. Heller is director of the AID
Office of Development Programs, Bureau for Latin
American Affairs, in Washington, D.C.

8

**PROMOTING
LATIN AMERICAN
INTEGRATION**

THE NATURE OF THE PROBLEM

It was shown earlier that the establishment of the IDB was the result of a surge of continental nationalism in Latin America that also expressed itself, at approximately the same time, in the Treaty of Montevideo and the Treaty of Managua, establishing the Latin American Free Trade Association (LAFTA) and the Central American Common Market (CACM), respectively. At first sight, it comes as a surprise that the word "integration" is not mentioned in the Agreement establishing the IDB. It should, however, be borne in mind that the Treaty of Montevideo was not signed until February, 1960, whereas the IDB Agreement had been signed in April, 1959, and had entered into force on December 30 of that year. Thus, the founders of the IDB were not yet sure of the form that economic cooperation might take within the region or of the role that the IDB should play in the integration process.

In the drafting committee that prepared the Agreement, Brazil proposed that one of the IDB's functions should be "to finance regional programs and projects that would promote the development, integration and complementarity of the economies of member countries." The Argentinian delegation proposed a much more general wording, to the effect that the IDB should become "a genuine instrument of inter-American cooperation."

These two approaches were merged in the final
text, which states that "the purpose of the Bank
shall be to contribute to the acceleration of the
process of economic development of the member countries, individually and collectively."[1] The Agreement
also defines one of the five principal functions of
the IDB as follows:

> to cooperate with the member countries to
> orient their development policies toward a
> better utilization of their resources, in
> a manner consistent with the objectives of
> making their economies more complementary
> and of fostering the orderly growth of their
> foreign trade.[2]

The IDB has sought to reconcile the objectives
of "individual" and "collective" development in the
conviction that the region as a whole would stand to
gain if there were a greater measure of interdepen-
dence and cooperation in the planning and execution
of development projects. The management of the IDB
has been especially articulate in drawing attention
to the imperative need for Latin American integration
and has often referred to the IDB as the "Bank for
Latin American Integration."

The IDB regards it as part of its responsibility
to interest member countries in particular projects
that could be undertaken independently or on a coordinated basis and that would not only contribute to
national development but, also, help in promoting regional integration. Special importance was attached
to the Bank's role in this respect at the meeting of
American Presidents at Punta del Este in April, 1967.
The Presidents called, at that time, for the progressive creation, beginning in 1970, of a Latin American
Common Market; emphasized the importance of laying
the physical foundations for integration through
multinational projects, notably in the fields of
transportation, telecommunications, and power; and
recommended that the IDB "should have additional resources in order to participate actively in the attainment of this objective."[3]

Many obstacles, however, have stood in the way
of effective regional cooperation. Neither the IDB
nor any other development financing institution could
very well make such cooperation an indispensable condition of granting a loan if it could be demonstrated
that, even in the absence of regional cooperation,
positive benefits would be derived from a project.
Since international agreement on specialization is
notoriously difficult to achieve among developed and
developing countries alike, insistence on such agreement as a condition of assistance might be tantamount
to denying such assistance altogether.

One of the shortcomings of both the Treaty of
Montevideo and the Treaty of Managua is the much
greater emphasis placed on reducing tariffs--in an
effort to emulate the EEC--than on direct cooperation
in the development process. But, however effective
tariff cutting may have been in a region such as Europe, where a high level of development had already
been attained prior to the establishment of the EEC,
it could not provide equivalent impetus within a
group of underdeveloped countries faced with a quite
different set of problems.

Among the more advanced countries of Latin America, there was a fear that the opening up of regionwide markets might provide too great an incentive to
the large-scale foreign firms to come in and take
over key sectors of industry. In addition, among the
less developed countries, there was concern that the
benefits of integration were likely to accrue to the
stronger countries, rather than to the weaker ones.
Thus, it was not enough to reduce regional trade barriers; there was a need for some measure of joint
planning of industrial development that would provide
adequate incentives for both large and small countries
and for the less developed, as well as the more developed, nations. But this proved extraordinarily
difficult to achieve.

The result is that national development programs
and policies have generally been drawn up independently, without regard to their implications for one

another.   The LAFTA countries did agree to examine
their development programs together, with a view to
seeking a measure of harmonization.   But this has
remained only a long-term objective and has never
been implemented thus far in practice; member countries generally continue to move ahead with their industrial development without taking account of the
possibilities for regional specialization and exchange.   In Central America, a more serious effort
was made at joint planning, with the assistance of
a team to which the IDB, ECLA, and the OAS all contributed and which later became a department of the
Permanent Secretariat for Central American Economic
Integration (SIECA) of the CACM; but little was
achieved in terms of practical results.

In December, 1969, the member countries of LAFTA
adopted the Protocol of Caracas, prolonging the
transition period for the establishment of a free
trade area--which had been due to end in 1973 under
the Treaty of Montevideo--until December, 1980.   The
adoption of a common list of irrevocable tariff concessions was likewise postponed, pending agreement
on new arrangements for drawing up the list, which
were to be completed by the end of 1974.   Annual
tariff negotiations were to continue, but the objective was now to reduce each country's duties on imports from other LAFTA members by a weighted average
of only 2.9 per cent a year, as against the 8 per
cent a year originally envisaged under the Treaty of
Montevideo.

Meanwhile, a subgroup of LAFTA countries--con-
sisting of Bolivia, Chile, Colombia, Ecuador, and
Peru (Venezuela remaining uncertain whether to join)--
formed an association known as the Andean Group to
move ahead with economic integration much more rapidly
than appeared possible for LAFTA countries as a
whole.   They decided to accelerate the reduction of
mutual trade barriers, establish a common external
tariff, make effective provision for industrial specialization through complementarity agreements (which
are discussed further below), adopt a common policy
toward private foreign investment, and create an
Andean Development Corporation to undertake the

active promotion of integration projects. The Andean
Group also envisages a significant measure of joint
planning, and the IDB has offered its support for
this purpose.

THE IDB APPROACH

Notwithstanding the many obstacles to Latin
American integration, the IDB has sought to promote
this goal in several different ways. First and foremost, it has encouraged and financed specific projects
contributing to integration. Second, it has established a scheme for financing exports of capital
goods by Latin American countries to one another.
Third, it has created the Institute for Latin American Integration (INTAL) in Buenos Aires, which,
since 1965, has been undertaking research, training,
advisory, and information activities related to the
integration process. Fourth and finally, it has set
up a Preinvestment Fund for Latin American Integration, which, since 1966, has been financing general
and specific studies with a view to identifying and
formulating integration projects.

The total value of projects classified by the
IDB as contributing to economic integration amounted
to $514 million by the end of 1970. This amount
includes inter alia $310 million devoted to transpor-
tation, $68 million to electric power and telecommuni-
cations, and $54 million to the financing of intrare-
gional exports of capital goods. It cannot, however,
be assumed that the $378 million spent on infrastruc-
ture were devoted entirely to the objective of integration. For example, the entire cost of any road
crossing a national frontier was included in the
total, even though much of the traffic carried by
the road was likely to be concentrated within national boundaries.

Similar considerations apply to projects in the
field of telecommunications and electric power, in
which both the national and international aspects
of projects are classified by the IDB under the
heading of integration in the belief that investment

in the former is essential to the latter. For example, internal improvement of a telecommunications network is usually a precondition for the profitable operation of a ground satellite station or a terrestrial international connection.

The importance of establishing intercountry linkages in the fields of transportation, telecommunications, and power generation is evident. One of the greatest obstacles to the integrated development of the Latin American continent is the lack of internal lines of communication. The IDB has sought to help in breaking down the isolation of the individual countries from one another by financing the construction of international highways, such as those from the Paraguayan border to the Atlantic Ocean and from Valparaiso to Mendoza.

Through the Central American Bank for Economic Integration (CABEI), the IDB has been financing regional road-construction programs and a telecommunications network that will link the five Central American countries. The IDB has financed a prefeasibility report on the so-called Bolivarian Marginal Highway of the Jungle, an ambitious project that would link up the three principal river basins of South America-- the Amazon, the Orinoco, and the Plate--and is beginning to finance some short highway stretches of this proposed 3,700-mile road system. It has also agreed to finance a feasibility study of a road between Brazil and Peru that would ultimately link Brasilia to Lima.

Among the electric-power loans of significance for economic integration are those linking distribution systems in the state of Paraná in Brazil and the province of Misiones in Argentina with the IDB-financed Acaray hydroelectric power plant located in Paraguay. An important field for IDB financing is to be found in the cooperative development of river basins and frontier areas. River-basin development calls for a scale of resources normally beyond the capacity of individual countries.

Moreover, projects of this type may serve a whole variety of purposes, and it is important to be

able to strike the right balance between such purposes, with due regard to the legitimate interests
of all the bordering states. Among the aspects to
be considered are navigation, power generation, flood
control and irrigation, water supply, the protection
of river head waters, the development of access routes
to new areas and regions, and the building of infrastructure to permit the common exploitation of river-
basin resources and the creation of new poles of
development.

The first case of a project of this type was the
River Plate; a conference to consider the development
of this river was held as early as 1941. Any such
project, however, raises immense political, as well
as economic and technical, problems, and it was not
until 1965 that the governments of Argentina, Bolivia,
Brazil, Paraguay, and Uruguay agreed to ask the IDB
to do a preliminary study. This was duly undertaken
and published in 1969 in eight volumes and two
annexes.

The IDB is also studying possibilities for the
development of the Gulfs of Fonseca and Honduras and
of the River San Juan, all in Central America. The
Amazon and Orinoco are also clear cases for multinational river development if the requisite international agreements can be reached. Studies of the
integrated development of frontier areas have been
undertaken by the IDB, involving potential cooperation between Colombia and Venezuela, Colombia and
Ecuador, Argentina and Chile, Argentina and Bolivia,
and Costa Rica and Panama.

FINANCING MULTINATIONAL PROJECTS

The IDB has, from time to time, considered the
possibility of granting particularly favorable terms
for the financing of projects involving more than
one country of the region in order to facilitate the
process of regional integration. Thus far, the Bank
has concluded that it is not necessary to give special
terms, since there is sufficient flexibility within
the framework of FSO operations to permit adequate
financing in this field. On the other hand, specially

favorable terms are given by the Preinvestment Fund
for Latin American Integration for formulating multinational projects.

Since no multinational entities or enterprises
in Latin America have yet been formed to execute integration projects, IDB financing in this field has
had to take the form of individual loans, granted
simultaneously to the various countries concerned,
for the financing of any part of a multinational
project located in their respective territories. In
the various individual loan contracts, however, the
borrowers are required to follow certain procedures
for the coordination of investment and to adopt various financial and juridical measures to facilitate
the financing and execution of the projects.

For example, in the case of the hydroelectric
project at Acaray, which, as noted earlier, is to be
linked with the electrical networks of adjoining
areas in Argentina and Brazil, the IDB, in the first
instance, granted a loan to Paraguay for the construction of a generating plant; and disbursements related
to those parts of the project concerned with the generation and transmission of power for export to Argentina and Brazil were made conditional on the
signing of agreements by the latter two countries
regarding the linking arrangements to be made and the
conditions of purchase and sale. Later, the IDB
advanced loans to Argentina and Brazil for the building of transmission and distribution lines for power
from Paraguay, and, here again, expenditure of the
funds was made conditional on the signing of the
above agreements and on the carrying out of various
measures required to assure the success of the project.

INDUSTRIAL INTEGRATION

Compared with the funds made available for regional infrastructure, which account for over three-
quarters of total IDB lending for integration, the
resources allocated to productive enterprise have
been extraordinarily small--$22 million for industry
and $16 million for agriculture. The former figure

represents loans made to CABEI for industrial projects of regional scope, while the latter reflects
programs for the control of hoof-and-mouth disease,
requiring coordinated action by the recipient countries. This indicates the very limited progress thus
far made toward effective cooperation among the Latin
American countries under the Treaty of Montevideo.

In principle, the IDB has, for some time, been
applying a so-called integration criterion in project
evaluation, designed to indicate the extent to which
projects may contribute to the replacement of extra-
regional imports, make use of regional inputs or promote exports within the region, or help to create
the physical infrastructure for economic integration.
It has not, however, been possible to give major
weight to this criterion, because the countries themselves have not reached the stage of cooperation required.

In these circumstances, the IDB has had to
adopt a rather flexible and eclectic attitude and
has had to be content with trying to promote cooperative projects wherever possible and otherwise seeking to avoid projects that might tend to prejudice
the formation of a common market in the longer run.
The IDB's principal objective for industry has therefore been to encourage projects in which the scale
of production and level of productivity would make
it possible for the enterprises concerned not only
to cater to their respective national markets but,
also, to develop a substantial export capacity.

Among the projects that the IDB regards as
having contributed to regional cooperation in Latin
America are those for meat-processing and the production of speciality paper and cardboard in Argentina,
the extraction and pelletization of iron ore and the
production of refractory materials in Brazil, and
the manufacture of pulp and paper in Chile, sodium
carbonate in Colombia, vegetable oils in Paraguay,
cement in Uruguay, and fertilizer in Venezuela.

All these projects were established with the
deliberate intention of providing for an export

capability in addition to supplying the home market.
It does not, however, follow that they are integration projects in the sense of being part of a coher-
ent program of intercountry specialization. Similarly, the global loans given to various national
development institutions for modernizing small- and
medium-scale industry in order to reduce their unit
costs to internationally competitive levels would no
doubt be helpful in increasing the capacity of the
assisted industries to supply regionwide needs, but
these must be regarded as an indirect, rather than a
direct, form of assistance to integration.

More directly linked to the integration process
have been the global lines of credit given to CABEI
and the direct support to national programs of industrial development that the IDB has provided in the
case of Central America. These loans were for projects specifically designed to cater to the needs of
more than one country in the region or to utilize
raw materials, intermediate goods, or components supplied by other members of the CACM.

The IDB has not, however, been able to play the
role that it could have played in helping to develop
greater industrial specialization and exchange in
Latin America if the countries themselves had been
prepared to adopt effective measures for regional
cooperation. In the absence of such measures, the
IDB has had to operate at the fringes of the problem,
rather than at its center. What were needed were,
at the very least, some basic lines of agreement on
a distribution of industry policy for the Latin American region and, at best, a significant measure of
joint planning both for the economy as a whole and
for industry in particular.

Under the Treaty of Montevideo, provision was
made for working out a distribution of industry policy
through so-called complementarity agreements cover-
ing particular industries or industrial sectors on
a regionwide basis. According to LAFTA rules, a
complementarity agreement is designed to establish
a program of sectoral integration, through the liberalization of trade in the complementary products

of a particular industrial sector. It may also provide for harmonization of treatment accorded to imports from third countries.

Such harmonization may be applied not only to
products directly covered by the agreement--in order
to standardize preferential margins throughout the
LAFTA region--but, also, to raw materials and com-
ponents--so that manufacturers in one LAFTA country
should not gain an advantage simply by paying lower
tariffs on imports of raw materials and components
than do their competitors elsewhere in the region.
The agreement may also provide for coordination of
governmental programs and incentives designed to facilitate industrial complementarity and for special
advantages for the less developed countries.

Had it been possible to negotiate a large number
of such agreements, the IDB could have played a key
role by standing ready to finance the establishment
of new industries or the expansion of existing ones,
as required by the relevant agreements. The IDB
could have been particularly helpful in seeing to it
that the weaker and less developed countries were
given special aid in setting up industries capable
of supplying regionwide markets, so that they, too,
would have a stake in the process of industrial integration.

Too often, in the arrangements for regional cooperation among the developing countries that have
been negotiated, the weaker countries have tended to
get left behind. On the one hand, they have been
expected to discriminate in favor of imports from
their neighbors, even though this might mean paying
more for their imports than they would have done had
they purchased them in the United States or Western
Europe; and, on the other hand, they have been unable
to gain any industrial advantage for themselves, because, in a common market or free trade area, private
industry prefers to be located in the larger centers
in order to benefit from the services available in
such centers and from proximity to the markets that
they contain.

An important contribution could be made by the IDB in such cases by providing strong financial support in building up the industrial participation of the weaker and less developed countries. In several cases, not only in Latin America but, also, in other regions, failure to make adequate provision for the weaker members of regional groups has resulted in blocking efforts at cooperation and, in some cases, has led to an actual break-up of the groups concerned.

The character of the problem may be illustrated from experience in the CACM, which went further than LAFTA in seeking to evolve a distribution of industry policy for its region. The CACM developed three instruments to stimulate balanced industrial development—a System of Integration Industries, a Special System for Promotion of Productive Activities, and a Central American Agreement on Fiscal Incentives. None of these devices proved to be effective, with the result that an unbalanced pattern of intraregional trade and industrial investment emerged, to the detriment of the less developed countries. Notwithstanding the remarkable successes that were achieved in reducing intraregional trade barriers and increasing the volume of intraregional trade, the unequal distribution of benefits brought the CACM into a state of acute crisis and was an important factor in the outbreak of hostilities between Honduras and El Salvador in 1969.

The first of the above instruments, adopted in June, 1958, made special provision for so-called integration industries, defined as those industries needing access to the combined market of the whole Central American region because of the scale requirements of a plant of minimum efficiency. Arrangements were to be made whereby an equitable distribution of integration industries would take place among the member countries, and, in order to ensure this, it was provided that no country should be awarded a second integration industry until one such industry had been assigned to each of the other member countries.

The preference given to such industries was considerable, but not absolute; plants awarded integration-industry status were to enjoy immediate free access to the entire regional market, whereas any competing plant established elsewhere would be subject to the prevailing tariff, which would, however, be subject to annual linear reductions so that it, too, would enjoy free access at the end of ten years.

Agreements were reached in 1963 on a tire plant for Guatemala[4] and caustic soda and insecticide plants for Nicaragua, which were subsequently established. Requests have been made, but not thus far approved, for nylon plants for El Salvador and Guatemala, steel plants for Costa Rica and Honduras, and pulp and paper plants for Guatemala, Honduras, and Nicaragua.

Negotiations for the assignment of plants under this system proved to be cumbersome and difficult. In addition to political difficulties, lack of adequate infrastructure and managerial and financial resources posed serious problems. The rule requiring all countries to be awarded a plant before any country was assigned a second plant, designed as a means of ensuring equity, in fact presented a stumbling block.

It is not clear how far these difficulties might have been overcome if substantial external financial support had been forthcoming. If each country could have seen a reasonable prospect of receiving effective technical and financial assistance in setting up its own integration industries, it might have had fewer misgivings about surrendering a privileged position to corresponding plants established elsewhere.

In fact, however, the major national and international lending agencies, including the IDB, declined to support the basic idea involved[5] and were certainly unwilling to take initiatives in promoting integration-industry schemes with the governments

concerned. In their view, it was essential to maintain the kind of nondiscriminatory conditions in
which competition could operate, even where there
were large economies of scale. They were also concerned that the integration-industry approach would
interfere with the optimum location of industry.

Regarding the latter consideration, it has to
be borne in mind that members of a regional grouping
are likely to be prepared to make the adjustments required in opening their markets to the industries of
their neighbors only if they see compensating advantages for themselves. The concentration of new industries in the more advanced countries of Central
America has endangered the CACM by weakening the incentives to the less favored countries to stay in.

Industrial development is just as important an
ingredient in the development of the less advanced
countries, notably Honduras, as it is in Costa Rica
or El Salvador. If, therefore, one were to rely
solely on the free operation of market forces to
determine the location of industry in Central America
or in any other regional grouping, one would be running the risk of disintegration of the group, rather
than of integration.

There is more force in the contention that regional monopolies might hold the member countries of
CACM to ransom. On the other hand, in a region as
small and poor as Central America, it is almost inevitable that there may not be room in certain industries for more than one or two plants, if advantage
is to be taken of the economies of scale. It would
be no solution to the development problems of Central
America to permit the squandering of resources on
the proliferation of competing plants within the
area, all operating at suboptimal rates of capacity
utilization. In any case, failure of the international lending agencies to support the integration-
industry approach (or some other means of achieving
the same end) would not necessarily prevent the
creation of monopolies; it might merely leave the
field open for foreign companies to set up the monopolies in question.

A more constructive approach would be to ensure
that any monopolies that might be established would
be subject to supervision, as was indeed provided
under the Central American agreement on this matter,
and that import duties would be lowered in cases
where monopolies were insufficiently responsive to
the public interest. An important opportunity was
thus lost for assisting Central America in developing
an industrial base through agreements that would
have sought to share the benefits equitably among the
participating countries, thereby avoiding the tensions that developed subsequently.

In 1965, the integration-industry approach was,
in effect, superseded by the Special System for Promotion of Productive Activities, under which special
protection was afforded to new industries installed
in the area. But whatever success this arrangement
had was confined to the national level--theproblem
of regional development and regional balance remained
unsolved. A Central American Agreement on Fiscal Incentives, approved in 1966, was not ratified until
1969 and was still not in force at the beginning of
1971 for lack of interpretative regulations. In
these circumstances, the member countries engaged in
disastrous competition with one another in offering
tax concessions to attract foreign industries--which
frequently consisted of nothing more than assembly
operations.[6]

During the second half of 1970, strenuous efforts
were made by the Central American countries to negotiate a modus operandi for dealing with the impasse
that had arisen in the CACM. It was envisaged that
a Fund for the Expansion of Industrial and Agricultural Production would be set up within CABEI from
contributions by member countries that were to be
proportional to the benefits derived from the CACM.
The Fund was to be used for correcting the imbalance
that had arisen within the region.

Excessive protection was to be reduced, and the
Central American Agreement on Fiscal Incentives was
to be brought into effective operation. Rules of
origin were to be drawn up to prevent abuse of the

common market arrangements through free circulation of imported goods with very little regional value added. Agricultural policies were to be coordinated.

Above all, renewed efforts were to be made to achieve an industrialization policy for the region under which basic industries would be set up in accordance with sectoral agreements among the participating countries. The assignment and location of these industries were to be a matter for decision by the Economic Council of the CACM.[7]

A similar sectoral approach was adopted by the Andean Group. Both here and in Central America, active support by external financing agencies, especially the IDB, would substantially improve the chances of success, both by making capital available for the new industries and by ensuring that all countries belonging to the respective regional groups would secure tangible benefits from their participation.

The problems faced by the international financing institutions in supporting joint industrial planning among groups of developing countries call for entirely new and imaginative approaches and probably, also, for new types of assistance. The financing of infrastructure, to which the bulk of the resources for integration has been allocated so far, is no doubt of considerable help, and its importance should not be underestimated.

It would nevertheless be possible for countries to agree on cooperation in the fields of road transportation, power transmission, and telecommunications without ever really getting to the heart of the matter, which is cooperation in the productive sectors, especially industry. For it is in the latter sectors that the benefits of a common market are to be found first and foremost. Western Europe had a highly articulated network of roads, railroads, air transportation, power transmission, and intercountry telecommunications long before the idea of a common market ever became a practical possibility.

It is therefore clear that, although the development of internal lines of transportation and communications are a necessary condition for regional cooperation, they are by no means a sufficient condition. Much more thought has to be given to the ways in which external resources can be brought to bear in encouraging industrial cooperation among developing countries. Particular attention is required to the need for assistance designed to promote industrial specialization and exchange, as well as to support the weaker countries effectively.

It is not sufficient for this purpose to develop industries with an export capacity. It goes without saying that export capacities are required in all the participating countries, but integration requires more than this. Regionwide agreement on at least the broad outlines of a distribution of industry policy, as contemplated in the CACM and in the Andean Group, would appear to be a most desirable, if not indispensable, feature of any serious integration program.

As noted earlier, the IDB allows the borrower to apply a margin of preference on bids submitted by local suppliers in the country in which a project is to be undertaken, as against foreign suppliers. The preferential margin is equal to the level of import duties in the borrowing countries, subject to a maximum of 15 per cent. The IDB is studying the possibility of allowing borrowers to extend this preferential treatment to goods supplied by other Latin American countries that are members of the same integration agreement. If such an extension of preference were made, it would no doubt help to stimulate additional intraregional trade.

EXPORT FINANCING

The export-financing program introduced by the IDB in 1963 is of vital significance for Latin American industrial integration. Its object is to ensure that the export credits offered by Latin American countries with respect to shipments of capital goods should be competitive with those offered by major suppliers to Latin America in the industrial countries. Initially, $30 million were allocated for this purpose, and, in 1968, the amount was raised to $40 million. The IDB scheme provides medium-term financing--from 180 days to five years--and can cover up to 70 per cent of the invoice value.

In order to participate, a country has to designate a suitable national agency capable of undertaking the financial transactions required and of ensuring that funds are used only for purposes covered by the program. To be eligible for financing, a product must have an import content from outside the region that is less than 50 per cent of the f.o.b. export price.

The program operates entirely through national agencies on the basis of lines of credit from the IDB. Initially, the system was introduced without any commissions, but, in 1966, the IDB began to impose a 1 per cent annual rate of commission on the nondisbursed portion of any credit line. The great bulk of the funds provided under the scheme up to the end of 1969 went to Mexico ($26.8 million), Brazil ($15.5 million), and Argentina ($8.0 million).

Although the scheme has been useful and has led to the development of export-credit agencies in a number of countries where they did not previously exist, the IDB is aware of a number of shortcomings. In the first place, export-credit insurance has been slow to develop in Latin America, and export-credit arrangements, however valuable, are of limited effectiveness in the absence of parallel insurance facilities. Potential exporters who are unable to obtain insurance are faced with the need to assume full responsibility for the repayment of the credit provided in the event of default by an importer.

In such circumstances, there is likely to be a preference for selling to the home market, where suppliers are more familiar with the creditworthiness of buyers. Systems of credit insurance have been

established only recently in Argentina, Brazil, Colombia, and Mexico, and, even here, they do not provide
as much coverage as is available in the industrial
countries. The reason for the slow development of
export-credit insurance facilities is the small volume, which allows little spreading of risks and makes
it uneconomic to obtain commercial coverage. Proposals for multinational coverage have run into
various difficulties.

A second shortcoming of the IDB scheme is that
it applies only to exports to Latin America. Although
this is the sector of trade that is important from
the standpoint of regional integration, it constitutes a serious limitation on the usefulness of the
scheme viewed in broader terms. A third difficulty
is that the IDB scheme covers only capital goods currently financed in world markets by medium-term
credit. But there are other goods, such as durable
consumer goods and intermediate products, that are
also supplied under medium-term credits in world
markets, and, here, the scheme is inadequate.

Finally, the financing of 70 per cent of the
invoice value is insufficient in many cases. The assumption underlying the IDB scheme was that the exporting country would contribute 10 per cent of the
finance required and that the importer would make a
down payment of 20 per cent. But, in some cases,
competitive schemes require down payments of only 10
per cent of the invoice value on an f.o.b. basis and
15 per cent on a c.i.f. basis; occasionally, the
down payment required is even lower. It has therefore become necessary for the national agencies to
be in a position to finance a major part of the 30
per cent of invoice value not covered by the IDB,
even though this may mean financing transportation
and insurance costs accruing to other countries.

While the case for expanding the scope of the
export-credit facilities has considerable merit when
seen in terms of the need to promote Latin American
exports both to the region itself and to the rest of
the world, it has to be borne in mind that the scheme
is, for the time being, principally of interest to

the most advanced countries, which have absorbed the
bulk of the funds available for this purpose. Although there appears to be a strong case for extend-
ing the coverage and financial scope of the scheme
in a manner that would remedy the shortcomings referred to earlier, it would be necessary to ensure
that this did not lead to any distortion in the
over-all distribution of IDB funds to its member
countries.

AGRICULTURAL INTEGRATION

The prospects for a division of labor in agriculture are even less promising than in industry. In
Latin America, as in Europe, the agricultural sector
is the most backward in the economy as a whole. In
the Treaty of Rome, which established the EEC, the
approach taken to agriculture was quite different
from that adopted in relation to industry, and it was
never envisaged that a freely competitive market in
agricultural commodities would be established. The
Treaty of Stockholm, which set up the European Free
Trade Association (EFTA), went even further and virtually excluded agricultural commodities.

It was thus not surprising that, in the course
of discussions that preceded the adoption of the
Treaty of Montevideo, it was pointed out that agriculture in Latin America would need to undergo profound changes--involving land reform and the application of modern techniques--before it could be expected
to face the pressures of regional competition. The
Treaty of Montevideo therefore provides for special
treatment for agriculture. Participating countries
were to coordinate their agricultural development
and their agricultural trade policies and would attempt to expand their mutual trade in agricultural
products. This was to be done "without disorganizing
the regular productive activities of each contracting
party."[8]

Consequently, participating countries were authorized, during the transition period, to limit
their imports of agricultural products to the amounts

required to bridge the gap between domestic production
and consumption and were allowed, to this end, to
take steps to equalize the prices of imported and
domestic products. Where consumption exceeded domestic production, countries were required to give
priority, "under normal competitive conditions," to
products originating in the territories of other participating countries, "due consideration being given
to the traditional flows of intra-area trade."[9]

In short, it would be unrealistic and, indeed,
harmful to contemplate the early establishment of a
competitive multinational market for agricultural
commodities in Latin America, and it would be wrong
to expect more of the Latin American countries than
the industrially advanced countries have been able
to achieve in this respect. Whatever gains might be
obtained in a competitive market for agriculture in
the very long run, the price to be paid in the short
and medium run would be quite excessive in terms of
additional unemployment and underemployment on the
land, and no responsible government could be expected
to entertain such an approach. What is required is
a policy of cooperation and coordination, rather than
of reducing trade barriers.

As previously noted, the only agricultural loans
formally classified by the IDB as part of its integration program are those totaling $16 million that were
advanced to a number of Latin American countries to
deal with hoof-and-mouth disease on a coordinated
and cooperative basis. Clearly, the experience of
working together on a common agricultural problem is
valuable to the countries concerned and later may
lead to cooperative efforts of a more far-reaching
character. As they stand, however, these projects
do not, of course, contribute directly to agricultural
specialization or to the promotion of agricultural
trade in the region.

From the latter point of view, certain other IDB
projects might be regarded as having some significance
for agricultural cooperation in the region. Such
projects would include those tending to promote the
expansion of output of exportable commodities, which

might ultimately lead to a larger volume of regional
trade in these commodities. There are substantial
opportunities for such trade, since Latin America
continues to import agricultural products from outside the region valued at some $600 million a year.
Given effective planning and cooperation, it should
be possible to produce these commodities within the
region, thereby releasing scarce foreign-exchange
resources for other purposes.

The IDB has also been promoting joint programs
of agricultural research and technological adapta-
tion--notably at the Agrarian University at Lima,
Peru, and at the National School of Agriculture at
Chapingo, Mexico--and training programs of regional
scope--at the International Center for Tropical Agriculture in Colombia and at the International Center
for Corn and Wheat Improvement in Mexico. The IDB's
efforts to encourage the development and conservation
of forests and fisheries in Latin America should
also make an important contribution to the expansion
of intraregional trade in wood and fish products.

PREINVESTMENT FUND FOR LATIN
AMERICAN INTEGRATION

The Preinvestment Fund for Latin American Integration was established under a decision of the Board
of Governors of the IDB adopted in July, 1966. The
objective of the Fund is to identify countries or
regions offering opportunities for multinational investment and to define criteria for regional investment policies in various economic sectors. Up to
the end of 1969, the Fund had been allocated $19.5
million, of which $15 million came from the FSO,
$3.5 million from the SPTF, and $1.0 million from resources of the IDB allocated to technical assistance.
In 1969, the Governors recommended an increase in
the Fund's resources of $2 million a year for 1970-72.

The IDB uses the Fund for financing preinvestment studies in the fields of regional infrastructure; the integrated development of geoeconomic areas
cutting across national frontiers; the establishment

of basic industries on a regional scale; the joint
exploitation of national resources; scientific and
technical research, with exchange of information;
technical training; and the mobilization of human resources.

Among the projects financed with the Fund's resources are a series of preinvestment studies of the
interlinking of the domestic telecommunications systems of individual Latin American countries with each
other and with the rest of the world. The IDB is
carrying out these studies in cooperation with the
UNDP, for which it acts as executing agency. The
UNDP is contributing $955,400 to the studies, the IDB
is putting up $250,000, and the fifteen participating
countries[10] are contributing $529,000.

The Fund has also initiated studies designed to
identify projects that should be included within the
program for the integrated development of the River
Plate basin, as well as a study of the feasibility
of building a port on the Paraguay River, which would
open up new routes for Bolivian trade with Argentina,
Brazil, Paraguay, and Uruguay and provide an additional outlet to the sea for Bolivia. Studies have
been undertaken to examine the possibility of connec-
ting the electric-power systems of Argentina and
Uruguay, to determine the possibility of building a
power project on the Uruguay River between Argentina
and Uruguay, and to build three main Brazilian highways along the Brazil-Uruguay frontier.

The Fund has further supported studies by LAFTA
and The Brookings Institution. The former has produced studies for complementarity agreements in the
following industries: steel, pulp and paper, petro-
chemicals, fertilizer, motor vehicles, diesel motors
and tractors, artificial fibers, aluminum, ceramics,
and refractory materials. The latter project has
involved the coordination of the work of a group of
Latin American institutes on the location and optimum
size of plants that would produce special steels,
agricultural equipment, milk products, and plate
glass.

A major program currently under way with the Fund's resources is the drawing up of an inventory of multinational physical infrastructure projects in Latin America relating to transportation, communications, electric power, and international watersheds. This is designed to help countries and financial institutions identify projects that they might undertake, independently or on a coordinated basis, to meet both national requirements and the needs of integration. Apart from these and other activities of the Preinvestment Fund for Latin American Integration, the IDB is supporting a wide range of training, research, advisory, and information services on the integration process through various agencies in Latin America and through INTAL.

THE BALANCE-OF-PAYMENTS EFFECTS
OF IMPORT LIBERALIZATION

There is one type of financing activity in support of regional cooperation that lies entirely outside the scope of the IDB as presently constituted. This involves the provision of assistance to countries that encounter balance-of-payments difficulties as a result of the lowering of trade barriers within a regional grouping. Part of the hesitation of Latin American countries in liberalizing their imports from one another has been due to the fear that such liberalization would expose them to additional pressures on their balance of payments.

There is, therefore, a need for special accommodations to assist countries in meeting any temporary balance-of-payments difficulties resulting from lowering barriers to imports from their neighbors. The lack of such facilities has probably been one of the factors tending to obstruct progress toward a Latin American common market, since the liberalization of trade has thereby been made more difficult, as well as more risky, for participating countries than it need have been.

It is noteworthy that the Chilean delegation to the Quitandinha Conference in 1954 had proposed the following functions for an inter-American bank:

(a) the financing of development;

(b) dealing with temporary disequilibria
     in the balance of payments within
     limits as to quantity and security that
     should be carefully studied;

(c) contributing, to a predetermined ex-
     tent, in mitigating the effects of
     sharp declines in the prices of non-
     perishable basic products, through the
     provision of lines of credit against
     the collateral of these products.[11]

Clear priority was given to the development objective,
but it was suggested that, so long as the achievement
of this primary objective was not prejudiced thereby,
it might be possible to envisage action to deal with
temporary disequilibria, thereby complementing the
activities of the IMF; such action was to be limited
to cases in which balance-of-payments difficulties
resulted from factors beyond the control of the countries concerned, such as declines in their exports
or export prices.[12] The third function was envisaged
by Chile as being undertaken only "at a later stage,"
after the IDB had established itself and gained experience in the other activities proposed.

    In the outcome, the IDB was not authorized to
carry out the second and third of the above functions,
which probably reflects the view that this would have
conflicted with, rather than complemented, the activities of the IMF. Subsequently, in 1963, the IMF
introduced a compensatory financing facility to meet,
in part, the needs envisaged in the second function
proposed for the IDB by Chile.

    The limitation of IDB functions to long-term
loans for development projects has, however, involved
curtailing, in one important respect, the ability of
the IDB to support the integration process. In other
words, the IDB has not been in a position to give financial support to regional trade liberalization. It

is true that countries in balance-of-payments difficulties always have access to the IMF. But, where a
country has already made drawings on the IMF for
other purposes, it may be reluctant to seek further
credit from that organization if the granting of such
credit is likely to be accompanied by a request for
a significant change in the government's economic
program.

     In such a situation, where a country is forced,
in effect, to choose between liberalizing its imports
under an integration agreement and maintaining the
momentum of its economic program, it would almost
invariably choose the latter course rather than the
former. It is for this reason that a separate import-
liberalization facility is needed outside the scope
of the normal IMF credit tranches (in the same way
that the IMF itself provides compensatory financing
and buffer-stock facilities outside the credit
tranches). In view of its general responsibilities
for promoting Latin American integration, it would be
natural for the IDB to undertake a task of this type.[11]

SUBREGIONAL FINANCING

     It was suggested in Chapter 1, above, that one
of the main reasons for the establishment of the IDB
was the expectation that a regional development bank
would be able to come closer to the problems of the
region and react more sensitively to its needs.
Similar reasoning can be applied to subregional group-
ings of countries, and, in Latin America, there now
exist, in addition to the IDB itself, three subregional financing institutions.

     The first of these was established for the CACM--
CABEI, which has received funds from the IDB, as well
as from other sources. More recently, a regional
bank was established for the Caribbean in 1970, known
as the Caribbean Development Bank (CARIBANK); and,
as noted earlier, an Andean Development Corporation
has been created as an integral part of the Andean
Group. (A proposal has also been made for the creation of a financing mechanism for the six riparian
countries of the River Plate basin.)

The creation of such subregional institutions
clearly meets a real need insofar as it becomes possible to specialize in the integration problems of
smaller areas and smaller-scale borrowers and to give
them more careful and continuous attention than would
be feasible in a larger and more-complex agency. At
the same time, the existence of several layers of
multilateral institutions, often reaching down to
several further layers of national financing institutions, may tend to generate an administrative com-
plexity and congestion that could constitute a problem
in itself. This is not, however, the place to enter
into a fundamental reconsideration of the structure
of multilateral financing, especially since an examination of this problem could not be undertaken without going deeply into the outlook for bilateral
financing as well.

THE FUTURE

A major obstacle standing in the way of progress
toward a Latin American common market is the fear on
the part of many Latin American businessmen, as well
as trade unions and workers, that the opening up of
regionwide markets would provide additional incentives to foreign companies to expand their activities
in Latin America and, in many cases, take over or
overwhelm existing Latin American industries. It is
argued that Latin American enterprise stands little
chance of holding its own against the foreign companies, since, even where Latin American firms are
competitive on a worldwide scale, they do not possess
the immense resources and market power of their foreign competitors.

It would be of little use, as Latin American
countries see it, to open up regionwide markets in
the interests of greater efficiency if all the benefits of that efficiency were to accrue to foreign
enterprise. If regional integration is to make any
sense in terms of Latin America's long-term development, it will be necessary for any expansion of international business activity within the region to
be matched by an at least comparable expansion of
indigenous enterprise.

As matters now stand, however, there is no means of ensuring that this is what would happen within an integrated regional market.[14] Indeed, the preference of external lending agencies for approaches to a common market that stress the free play of market forces, rather than any effort to control the evolution of those forces through a distribution of industry policy, has convinced many Latin American industrialists and workers that they should not rush too hastily into unplanned and uncontrolled regional schemes.

These considerations have prompted the countries belonging to the Andean Group not only to attempt a measure of joint industrial planning but, also, to introduce a common policy for the treatment of foreign capital. Apart from reserving certain sectors for domestic enterprise alone, the common policy provides for the progressive transformation of foreign companies, within a specified period of time--fifteen to twenty years--into mixed or domestically owned companies through the sale of equity to the nationals of the country concerned.[15]

As a bank relying largely on resources supplied by the U.S. Government and private investors, however, the IDB has, no doubt, been reluctant to promote dirigiste solutions to the integration problem in Latin America. It has preferred to follow the less controversial route of trying to build up regional infrastructure--which is bound to be needed anyway and which was strongly advocated by the meeting of American Presidents at Punta del Este in April, 1967 --while avoiding the touchy problems connected with the development of industries catering to regionwide markets. The problem therefore remains of how to harness IDB resources effectively to a more-rapid growth of regional industry in a manner that will at once avoid the take-over of the commanding heights of the Latin American economy by foreign companies and will distribute the benefits equitably among the participating countries.

In the Andean subregional agreement, member countries are seeking to establish distribution of industry policies involving coordinated investment programs by industrial branches or sectors. (Similar policies would have been adopted by the Central American countries, had the negotiations for a _modus operandi_ succeeded, as described earlier.)

If successful, this approach would facilitate the balanced industrial development of the region and, at the same time, take advantage of the economies of scale resulting from market expansion. This provides an important opportunity for the international lending institutions, including the IDB, to review the basic assumptions of past policies and to adjust them, in order to permit vigorous support for new efforts in cooperative region-building, along lines acceptable to the weaker, as well as the stronger, members of the grouping.

NOTES

1. IDB, _Agreement_, Art. I, sec. 1.

2. _Ibid._, Art. I, sec. 2 (a)(iv).

3. IDB, _Eighth Annual Report, 1967_ (Washington, D.C., 1968), p. 10.

4. A tire plant was also installed in Costa Rica, which, however, received the nonpreferential treatment described above.

5. According to Raymond F. Mikesell, both the IDB and AID refused to sanction the use of funds lent to CABEI for financing firms given integration-industry status. See his article "External Financing and Regional Integration," in Miguel S. Wionczek, ed., _Latin American Economic Integration_ (New York, 1966), p. 202.

6. See _Comercio Exterior_ (Mexico: Banco Nacional de Comercio Exterior, S.A.), September, 1970, p. 730.

7. _Ibid._, p. 729. The adoption of the above program was frustrated by continuing friction between

Honduras and El Salvador, as a result of which El
Salvador declined to support the new Fund. In December, 1970, Honduras, in effect, suspended its membership in the CACM by decreeing the application of the
common external tariff to all imports by Honduras,
with certain specified exceptions.

8. Treaty of Montevideo, Art. 27. English text
of treaty can be found in Sidney Dell, A Latin American Common Market? (New York: Oxford University
Press, 1966), pp. 228-56.

9. Treaty of Montevideo, Art. 29.

10. Argentina, Barbados, Bolivia, Brazil, Chile,
Colombia, the Dominican Republic, Ecuador, Haiti,
Panama, Paraguay, Peru, Trinidad and Tobago, Uruguay,
and Venezuela. The telecommunications systems of
these countries will also be linked to those of Mexico
and Central America, currently under construction.

11. Statement of Arturo Maschke, President of
the Central Bank of Chile, to the Subcommittee on
the Financing of Development, Quitandinha Conference,
as cited in Arturo Maschke, La Creación del Banco
Interamericano de Desarrollo (Mexico D.F.: Centro
de Estudios Monetarios Latinoamericanos, 1966), p. 91.

12. Ibid., p. 93.

13. There is no reason, even from an orthodox
banking point of view, why a single institution
should not handle short-term, as well as medium- and
long-term, loans. The creation at Bretton Woods of
the IMF and the World Bank as separate institutions
was sharply criticized, at the time, by the American
Bankers Association and the First National Bank of
New York, both of which felt that the IMF should have
been set up as a department of the World Bank. See
U.S., Congress, House, Committee on Banking and Currency, Hearing on H. R. 2211, Bretton Woods Agreements
Act, 79th Cong., 1st sess., 1945, II, 349-51 and 406.

14.   In his letter of resignation as Secretary-General of the CACM, dated July 18, 1970, Carlos Manuel Castillo noted that "foreign investment has not always been directed towards supplementing domestic savings or facilitating the transfer of technology; it has often displaced Central American enterprise, or has served merely as a means of maintaining existing channels of supply to the markets." _Comercio Exterior_ (Mexico: Banco Nacional de Comercio Exterior, S.A.), September, 1970, p. 732.

15.   _Ibid._, February, 1971, pp. 114 _et seq._

9

The Charter of Punta del Este and the Act of Bogotá recognized that Latin American development calls for fundamental economic and social reform and structural change. The IDB is not, cannot be, and should not be the agent of such change or reform. It is the servant of its member governments, not their master. It has therefore been a point of some importance with the IDB that the final responsibility for decisions on the formulation of plans, definition of policies, establishment of priorities, and adoption of investment decisions must rest with the member countries and that IDB loans should not be used as a means of exerting pressure in these matters.

Within its framework of activity and terms of reference, the IDB has established an impressive record of achievement and innovation. From 1961 to 1970, it authorized 622 loans totaling $4.1 billion, against which it disbursed $2.2 billion. The fears expressed at the time of its establishment that funds channeled through the IDB would be at the expense of other assistance to Latin America have not been realized. The average annual flow of resources to Latin America from multilateral sources rose from $56 million in 1951-60 to $389 million in 1968-70, while the corresponding increase from bilateral sources was from $194 million to $750 million. In other words, the IDB has helped in the achievement of a major objective of its founders--namely, to expand substantially the over-all flow of capital to Latin America.

One-quarter of the funds lent by the IDB between 1961 and 1970 went into the improvement of agriculture and the opening up of new land. A similar proportion was devoted to social projects, particularly sanitation and housing. One-sixth was allocated to industry. And 30 per cent was supplied to the more-traditional objects of multilateral financing--the building of power and telecommunications systems, the construction of roads, and the modernization of ports.

The IDB is potentially subject to greater influence from its debtors than almost any other lending agency, national or international. The United States does, of course, have a predominant voice on major issues, as well as a decisive voice on the use of FSO resources--a result of the very large proportion of IDB financing contributed by the United States either through direct subscriptions or through the purchase of IDB bonds.

But the Latin American countries have nevertheless been able to achieve a significant number of their objectives for the IDB's operations. This being the case, it says much for the effectiveness of the IDB as a regional development institution and for the diplomatic skills of its top management that U.S. support has been enlisted for a large expansion of the IDB's activity--from an average annual rate of about $280 million in 1961-64, in terms of commitments, to a level of over $600 million in 1969-70.

As the financial commitment of the United States to the IDB has expanded, increasing attention has been paid to the policy framework within which the Bank operates and to the efficiency with which it deploys its resources. On the one hand, growing emphasis has been placed, especially since 1967, on policy coordination with the World Bank, the IMF, and AID, both directly and through the machinery of CIAP. On the other hand, efforts have been made to

strengthen the IDB's machinery for evaluation and
control, in order to ensure that the highest administrative standards are maintained. At the same time,
there has been evidence of increasing Congressional
concern in the United States regarding multilateral
lending programs in general and the program of the
IDB in particular.[1]

There are strong grounds for the recommendation
of the Pearson Commission that the share of the multilateral agencies in the total flow of resources to
developing countries should be increased very substantially. Potentially, the international character
of these agencies would enable them to deal with the
problems of lending for development without regard
to any consideration other than the best interests
of the developing countries themselves. The question,
however, is whether this undoubted potential can be
realized in practice. A senior official of AID has
pointed out that one of the arguments against increasing the share of multilateral agencies in the
U.S. aid program is that this

> could destroy the multilateral character of
> these entities by the sheer weight of dis-
> proportionately large U.S. contributions.
> Thus, it would have the reverse effect of
> that anticipated, by "politicizing" these
> institutions. They also point out that,
> while our Congress has so far refrained
> from imposing restrictive conditions on
> U.S. contributions to multilateral bodies,
> there is a high probability that this re-
> straint would disappear if our assistance
> became much more heavily concentrated in
> these international entities. This would
> mean that our appropriations to these en-
> tities would be weighted with many legis-
> latively imposed procedural and administra-
> tive barnacles of the sort which now encum-
> ber our bilateral programs.[2]

The concerns expressed in these observations find
justification in conflicts that have arisen within
the IDB in connection with loans to certain countries.[3]

Moreover, a critical situation arose in 1971, when the U.S. Congress failed to appropriate the full amount of an installment due on a subscription to the ordinary capital of the IDB that it had previously authorized the U.S. Governor of the IDB to commit in a multilateral negotiation. As the U.S. Under-Secretary of the Treasury pointed out at the time, such action in breach of an international commitment was bound to damage the ability of U.S. representatives "to negotiate convincingly and advantageously in the future."[4] It also raised the most serious and fundamental questions regarding the whole basis on which the multilateral agencies operate. As the Under-Secretary put it, "International cooperation can thrive on the healthy bargaining involved in the negotiation process; it cannot survive the prospect of perpetual renegotiation."[5]

Another potential source of difficulty was the provision adopted by Congress at the end of 1970 whereby every new loan by the IDB, as well as by the World Bank, IDA, and the ADB, was to be the subject of special reports by the National Advisory Council on International Monetary and Financial Policies that were to indicate how each loan would benefit the people of the recipient country and whereby, in the case of the IDB only, reports were to be submitted on steps taken by IDB members to restrain military expenditures and strengthen "free and democratic institutions."[6]

It is clearly not possible to do more than speculate about how serious the dangers implicit in the foregoing developments might prove to be and how far they might be damped down by the counterweighting of interests of other donor countries in the event that Canada and other developed countries were admitted to membership, as was envisaged in a proposed amendment to the IDB Agreement introduced toward the end of 1971.

Another source of concern about the channeling of aid through the multilateral agencies is not inherent in such channeling, but arises only from the

particular circumstances in which this would be likely
to take place. Some of the most influential supporters of a shift to multilateral assistance do not base
their views on a belief in the superiority of the
multilateral approach, but see such a shift as providing an opportunity for further reducing the aggregate volume of aid furnished by the United States
through all channels combined. There is, of course,
no reason to suppose that efforts to curtail aid
programs would be less effective if the present
bilateral/multilateral distribution were maintained.

From the standpoint of its influence on international assistance policy, the greatest successes
of the IDB were achieved during its early years and
even during the period of international debate that
preceded its establishment. Among the concepts accepted solely or partially in the context of the international discussions and negotiations that led up
to the founding of the IDB[7] were the following:

   (1)   The advantages of a regional bank in
        specializing in the problems and re-
        quirements of a particular region or
        subregion, in being staffed largely by
        nationals of the countries in that re-
        gion, and in evolving an especially
        close relationship and rapport with its
        member countries;

   (2)   The need for multilateral lending agen-
        cies to advance beyond the stage of
        acting merely as passive channels for
        the flow of private resources to the
        developing countries under interna-
        tional guarantee and to assume the
        functions of fully fledged interna-
        tional development institutions capa-
        ble of taking a broad biew of the de-
        velopment requirements of their member
        countries, involving promotional, tech-
        nical-assistance, and preinvestment ac-
        tivities, in addition to straight finan-
        financing;

(3)   The importance of providing multilateral
      agencies with the capacity for adjusting
      the terms of lending to the debt-ser-
      vicing capacity of member countries,
      notably through the creation of soft-
      lending facilities obtained from gov-
      ernment subscriptions;

(4)   The need for a multilateral agency em-
      powered to lend to Latin American pri-
      vate enterprise without guarantee and
      to provide equity capital[8];

(5)   The need to diversify the lending oper-
      ations of the multilateral agencies and
      enable them to move beyond infrastruc-
      ture projects into the financing of
      directly productive activities, notably
      in the fields of agriculture and indus-
      try;

(6)   The key role of social projects in
      strengthening the development process
      and in effecting a wider distribution
      of the benefits of development and the
      scope for activity by the multilateral
      agencies in giving financial and tech-
      nical support to projects in the fields
      of education, health, urban development,
      housing, and the provision of drinking
      water and sewage systems;

(7)   The need for a mechanism that would
      make it possible for multilateral agen-
      cies to reach not merely large-scale
      enterprise but small- and medium-scale
      farmers and industrial entrepreneurs
      as well;

(8)   The importance, in this context, of de-
      centralizing the lending process by
      supplying resources to national devel-
      opment banks and other local financial
      institutions for re-lending to domestic
      enterprises;

(9)   The possibilities for enhancing the ef-
      fectiveness and flexibility of lending
      programs by not limiting assistance to
      import financing, but by standing ready
      to defray local costs wherever this
      would encourage the supply of domesti-
      cally produced raw materials, compon-
      ents, equipment, transport facilities,
      or other inputs;

(10) The potentially strategic significance
      of regional banks in supporting coop-
      eration among member countries, with a
      view to harmonizing their patterns of
      growth and investment, taking advantage
      of opportunities for specialization and
      exchange, and creating regionwide mar-
      kets for national industries.

The acceptance of the need for soft-lending facilities resulted not merely in the establishment of
the FSO as an integral part of the IDB but, also, in
the creation of IDA within the framework of the World
Bank. The unwillingness of contributing countries
to expand IDA resources in line with requirements,
however, and the consequent severe limitation on
Latin American access to IDA facilities (particularly
in view of the priority claims of low-income countries in Asia and Africa) placed a correspondingly
greater burden of responsibility on the IDB in this
respect. The result is that two-thirds of IDB lending is currently made available through the FSO.

Regarding the provision of resources for small-
and medium-scale enterprises, it would clearly have
been cumbersome, inefficient, and, therefore, uneconomic for the IDB to try to deal with a multitude of
small loans all over Latin America. This part of
the IDB's program was therefore carried out by making
so-called global loans to some fifty development
banks and institutions located in the various member
countries. These global loans reached an aggregate
level of $788.6 million by the end of 1969, equiva-
lent to 23 per cent of the total lending activity of
the IDB. Of this amount, $385.7 million came from

the ordinary resources of the IDB, mainly for industrial projects; $399.7 million from the FSO/SPTF,
largely for agriculture; and the remaining $3.2 mil-
lion from Canadian and United Kingdom funds.

This decentralization of the lending process is
a very significant feature of IDB activity, which
offers an important avenue for an expansion of multilateral lending operations in the future. Although
there has been no tendency, thus far, for the share
of "indirect" lending in total IDB operations to
rise, such an increase would become particularly important if it were intended to channel a larger proportion of total official resources through the
multilateral agencies.

With the passage of time, the differences between
the IDB and the World Bank have narrowed appreciably,
each institution having adopted ideas and practices
from the other. On the one hand, the World Bank,
apart from establishing a soft-lending affiliate--
IDA--has diversified its operations, in order to increase its support of such sectors as agriculture,
industry, education, water supply, and sewage systems, as well as power, transportation, and telecommunications, which had accounted for nine-tenths of
its activity in Latin America during the 1950s.

The World Bank, like the IDB, also lends to national development banks, agricultural credit institutions, and other financial intermediaries in cases
where intimate knowledge of local conditions is important and the scale of individual projects is too
small to make direct loans possible. Above all, the
World Bank now regards itself as a development agency
and has taken a number of initiatives associating
itself with the development problems of its members
and proposing methods for their solution, including
the provision of the necessary financial resources.

On the other hand, the IDB has, in recent years,
moved into the financing of large-scale infrastructure projects along lines similar to the World Bank;
and, although it has maintained its interest in industry and social projects, the relative and, in some

cases, absolute level of its activities in these
areas has receded. Moreover, as the scale of IDB
operations has increased, closer coordination with
the activities and policies of other lending agencies
has been sought through the machinery of CIAP. Since
1967, the IDB has undertaken, when programing the
use of its resources, to take account of the development efforts of its members, as assessed by CIAP,
and to help in overcoming deficiencies in such efforts. Member countries have been advised that "severe performance problems"--such as inadequate fiscal,
monetary, or administrative policies--may lead to a
reduction in IDB lending.[9]

Notwithstanding the convergence of the policies
of the multilateral agencies in recent years, the
IDB retains a certain individuality as a result of
its background, its character as a regional bank
closely associated with the views and aspirations of
its member countries, and the composition of its
staff and top management. Although it subscribes
fully to the CIAP objective of seeking to improve
the performance of its members, its regional character compels it, to some extent at least, to try to
maintain a certain balance in the allocation of its
resources among its members.

The experience of the 1960s suggests a number
of respects in which IDB operations could be made
more effective. The IDB, like the World Bank, faces
a growing incompatibility between the cost of loans
out of its ordinary resources and the debt-servicing
capacity of its members. The IDB is, in some ways,
in an even more difficult position than the World
Bank on this score, partly because, owing to its more
recent establishment, the average cost of the borrowed
resources available to it is higher than the corresponding cost of funds in the hands of the World Bank
and partly because the IDB has to charge its borrowers a 1.25 per cent premium over its own borrowing
rate; whereas the World Bank, with its much stronger
reserve position built up over a longer period, has
been able to lend at a rate fractionally below its
average borrowing rate. Equally serious is the fact
that desirable changes in policy are sometimes ruled

out for fear of the repercussions (real or imaginary)
upon international capital markets. Only by virtue
of the large-scale funds subscribed by governments
to the FSO has the IDB been able to adjust the terms
of its lending to the debt-servicing capacity of its
members.

The IDB and the World Bank have already moved
several steps away from the Bretton Woods concept of
multilateral lending, in which development requirements were only incidental and the main emphasis was
on ensuring the security of international bond flotations. The need for a further step is clearly indicated, because the terms of borrowing from the
ordinary resources of the IDB and the World Bank
have had to be determined not by considerations relating to the debt-servicing capacity and available
resources of the borrowing countries but by factors
arising out of economic policies pursued by the industrial countries for the achievement of domestic
objectives.

There would clearly be an advantage in a deliberate recognition that the primary function of the
multilateral agencies is to act as channels for the
flow of official funds, while the contribution of
private funds raised at market rates should be regarded as supplementary and should not interfere
with the adoption of policies considered desirable
on grounds of development needs. Private funds, in
any case, contribute only one-sixth of the total resources of the IDB, or one-quarter of its resources
in convertible currency.

It is sometimes asserted that the access of
the multilateral agencies to private capital markets
gives them an important degree of freedom that they
would not have if they depended entirely on government subscriptions. Such freedom may, however, be
more apparent than real. Governments can withhold
permission for the sale of bonds in their capital
markets just as readily as they can reduce their
subscriptions. Moreover, the borrowing capacity of
the IDB and the rating of its bonds depend on the
callable capital subscribed by the United States, so

that a failure to replenish such capital in the
amounts required, as occurred in 1971, is just as
effective a brake on IDB operations as curtailment
of subscriptions to the paid-in capital or to the
FSO would be.

A further evolution of the concept of multilateral assistance should also make it possible to envisage the provision of grants by multilateral
agencies, as well as loans. There is nothing about
the concept of a grant that requires that it be
given only as part of a bilateral program. Grants
out of net income are already provided by the IDB
and the World Bank for technical assistance, while
the World Bank makes grants out of net income to
IDA. Similarly, the resources of the UNDP are given
entirely in the form of grants for technical assistance and preinvestment.

A more flexible approach to the transfer of resources would make it possible for the multilateral
agencies to adjust their programs more precisely to
the requirements of their member countries. Some of
their members are in a position to pay market rates
for borrowed resources, while others are either so
poor or in such a difficult situation resulting from
past accumulations of debt on inappropriate terms
that they ought to be candidates for grants-in-aid.

A second improvement would be to authorize the
IDB, as well as the World Bank, to undertake nonproject lending, for the reasons discussed in Chapter
7, above. Some officials of the multilateral agencies are of the opinion that they can achieve all
the desirable objectives of nonproject lending by
local cost financing. This, they believe, would enable them to retain simultaneously the advantages of
project financing, notably the institution-building
and transfer of skills and techniques that go together with such financing. Clearly, it would be
better to handle the matter in this way in preference
to not handling it at all. But it would be better
still to deal with the issue directly, rather than
in a roundabout way through local cost financing.

For one thing, since local cost financing is tied in with project financing, it has the same inflexibility as does project financing and, in particular, cannot be readily adjusted to short-term needs or disbursed promptly in the light of a pressing requirement, such as may be caused by a shortfall in the export proceeds of a country or the emergence of excess capacity. Second, the distribution of assistance between project and nonproject financing should be considered as a priority question in itself, a question that should be settled on its own merits and not indirectly as a by-product of the local cost-financing requirements of particular projects.

As for local cost financing, there is a need for an altogether more flexible approach, as recommended by the Pearson Commission. Present local contribution requirements are greatly in excess of the level needed to assure a sense of participation and responsibility on the part of borrowers and are often onerous for the least developed countries. It is particularly important to avoid rigid formulae for local cost financing, since, as noted in Chapter 4, above, these tend to create incentives to choose certain types of projects that may be inconsistent with the priorities assigned to them in the national plan.

Moreover, the 15 per cent margin of preference for local suppliers applied by the IDB in common with the World Bank is entirely insufficient in view of the substantial capacity available in Latin America for construction projects and the production of capital goods. Preference should be given not merely to local suppliers but, also, to all Latin American producers within the framework of regional integration arrangements.

Special efforts are required to enlarge the volume of industrial financing by the IDB, which has fallen to inordinately low levels. Over the period 1961-70 as a whole, the IDB devoted only 15 per cent of its resources to industry, and, in 1970, the proportion was under 8 per cent: The Asian Development Bank, on the other hand, has allocated nearly 40 per

cent of its financing to industry. Part of the problem results from the inability of the IDB to lend
without guarantee or to undertake equity participation in an enterprise.

This problem could be resolved through the creation of a regional finance corporation to undertake
the same role for the IDB that the IFC performs for
the World Bank Group. Dangers of overlapping and
duplication are minimal, because of the enormous
scope for promotional activities in Latin America.
The arguments against a regional finance corporation
do not seem more persuasive in the present context
than were the corresponding arguments against the
IDB itself during the 1950s.

But the establishment of such a corporation
would not remove other sources of difficulty--namely,
the slow and cumbersome procedures of the IDB and
the consequent length of time (as much as three or
four years) taken before a sound financing proposal
culminates in actual disbursements. This factor is
also responsible for the continuing low level of
over-all disbursements in relation to over-all authorizations. Although a substantial part of the
delay is attributable to perfectly normal lags inherent in theworking out of any project, part is due,
also, to the elaborate checks and controls required
by the IDB in order to reduce risks to an absolute
minimum and thereby safeguard its own creditworthiness.

As long as the view is taken that a default on
a loan is the biggest disaster that could overtake
a multilateral development agency, so long will it
prove difficult, if not impossible, to adopt the
kind of vigorous and single-minded approach needed
in dealing with the development problem on the scale
and with the flexibility required. For there cannot
be development without risk-taking, and the multilateral agencies ought to be free to take product risks
without having to look constantly over their shoul-
ders at the possible reaction of the bond market or
of influential legislators. This is particularly
necessary if a much larger volume of funds is to be
channeled through these agencies and if they, in

turn, are to increase the proportion of indirect
lending, through financial intermediaries, to small-
and medium-scale enterprises.

Social projects have also been receiving a rapidly declining share of IDB financing at the same
time as the World Bank has been taking a greater interest in them. For example, the share of urban development and housing slumped to under 5 per cent of
IDB lending in 1968-70, while the World Bank, in
1970, announced the creation of a new division for
the consideration of projects of urban development.
Whether or not the IDB's emphasis on social projects
was excessive in the early 1960s and whether or not
some of these projects achieved only limited success,
the pendulum now appears to have swung too far against
such projects, and a rethinking of approaches in
this field seems called for.

The reaction against social projects and industry has led the IDB to devote much more attention to
massive infrastructure projects in the fields of
power and transportation, which had traditionally
been the specialty of the World Bank. The IDB hardly
seems to have a comparative advantage in projects of
this type, which do not make use, to the same extent,
of the Bank's close contacts with its member countries
and its familiarity with local conditions and requirements.

There is also a need for more effective activity
in support of regional integration. Here again, the
IDB cannot afford to be tied down to conventional
concepts of project financing. These are useful in
the development of regional infrastructure, but can
contribute little toward solving such problems as
the planning of industrial specialization, the implementation of a distribution of industry policy, and
the adoption of measures to protect the poorest countries and to assist weak industries to stand up to
greater competition. Although the slow progress of
Latin American integration is mainly the result of
government policy and there has been no lack within
the IDB of the will to support integration, there

is a need for new approaches to the problem by the
IDB, setting aside conventional notions and the drawing of simplistic parallels with European experience.

Finally, a great deal of clarification is needed
concerning the meaning of the IDB decision to adjust
the volume of its lending in the light of CIAP appraisals of country performance. In the first place,
it hardly seems appropriate to limit appraisals of
performance to fiscal, monetary, and administrative
aspects, since, as indicated by the Act of Bogotá
and the Charter of Punta del Este, basic reforms are
at least as important, if not more so. In the second
place, the measurement even of fiscal and monetary
performance is not at all as easy as some authorities
appear to believe. In particular, the only objective
indicators that are available do not distinguish the
"effort" made by a country from fortuitous success
(or failure) resulting from factors beyond its
control.

Moreover, even if objective indicators of pure
effort were available, it is not obvious that these
ought to be decisive in the allocation of aid. For,
in that case, aid would be distributed in proportion
to efficiency, which is a very different matter from
distributing it in accordance with considerations of
equity. It could even be argued that to back the
efficient is to support those who actually need assistance least.

There is, therefore, much to be said for the IDB
principle that had been applied in a straightforward
manner prior to 1967 and that has been subject to
important qualifications since--namely, the principle
that it is the obligation of a regional financing
institution to maintain a presence in, and flow of
assistance to, all its member countries. This at
once implies the application of different standards
to different countries, depending on such factors as
the stage of their development, the nature of the
obstacles confronting them, and the character of any
programs and priorities adopted by their responsible
authorities.

As noted earlier, steps have been taken toward offering membership in the IDB to Canada and other developed countries. Views differ about whether this would be consistent with maintaining the essential character of the IDB as a regional agency, staffed and run by the borrowers. On the one hand, the Latin American countries would be most reluctant to lose their majority voting position in the IDB. On the other hand, they recognize that the strength of their position may be more apparent than real in circumstances in which one member is able to determine the amount and distribution of FSO resources, as well as the borrowing capacity of the IDB.

Advantages are therefore seen in a diversification of membership among developed countries, so that the danger of domination by any one country is thereby reduced. Such diversification is also favored by the United States as a means of reducing its share of the burden of IDB financing. It is by no means certain, however, that the offer of membership in the IDB to European countries, Canada, and Japan would enlist substantially more resources from these countries, especially in view of the claims of African and Asian countries, many of which are much poorer than are most of the Latin American countries.

It will be clear, in summary, that, to some extent, the IDB has met the fate of any innovator--it has seen the innovations of the past become the orthodoxies of the present. Moreover, in proportion as its own role has been greatly enhanced, it has had to move more closely into line with the predominant thinking of the day on the matters with which it is concerned; and, as its rate of lending has advanced, it has had to pay increasing attention to the concerns of those providing the bulk of the external resources.

For the time being, the IDB is aware of conflicting pressures: of the need to reconcile innovation with orthodoxy and new ideas with conventional wisdom. The IDB has retained the intellectual capability, the institutional framework, and the close relationship with member countries required for new

creative thinking about the problems of development.
There are grounds for hoping that it also retains
the capacity and drive to translate new concepts into
new types of activity, to the extent that these prove
to be compatible with the inevitable constraints that
result from the manner in which its resources are
provided.

NOTES

1. See Chapter 3, above.

2. Jack Heller, "Development Assistance Strategies in Latin America," Development Digest, VIII, 3
(July, 1970).

3. See Chapter 7, above.

4. Statement of Charles E. Walker, Under-
Secretary of the Treasury, before the Subcommittee
on Foreign Operations of the Senate Appropriations
Committee, on fiscal year 1972 appropriations for
international financial institutions, June 8, 1971.

5. Ibid. For further details, see Chapter 3,
above.

6. Public Law 91-599 (H.R. 18306), ch. 3, approved on December 30, 1970, in Statutes at Large,
LXXXIV, 1657. For further discussion, see Chapter 3,
above.

7. Some would argue that the establishment of
the IDB was part of a much larger change in national
and international assistance policy, which took place
in the late 1950s and the early 1960s, and that it
would be incorrect to attribute all the ideas listed
below merely to the setting up of the IDB. That
there is much force in this view is indicated in
Chapter 1, where the various elements of the international debate and its outcome are brought together.
It would, indeed, be false to suggest that the IDB,
actual or projected, was the sole influence at work,
but certainly the activities of the Latin American
countries in pressing for this and other objectives
were of critical importance at the time.

250 THE INTER-AMERICAN DEVELOPMENT BANK

8. The IDB was not, in fact, given these powers; instead, the IFC was established within the framework of the World Bank.

9. IDB, <u>Proposal for an Increase in the Resources of the Inter-American Development Bank</u> (Washington, D.C., April, 1970), par. 3.10.

SELECTED BIBLIOGRAPHY

Avramovic, Dragoslav. "Latin American External Debt."
    Journal of World Trade Law, Vol. 4, No. 2
    (March/April, 1970).

Broide, Julius. Banco Interamericano de Desarrollo:
    Sus Antecedentes y Creación. Washington, D.C.:
    IDB, 1968.

Cordovez Zegers, Diego. El Banco Interamericano de
    Desarrollo. Santiago de Chile: Editorial Uni-
    versitaria, 1962.

Dell, Sidney. A Latin American Common Market? New
    York: Oxford University Press, 1966.

Gardner, Suzanne W., and Powelson, John P. "Regional
    Banking in the Americas." Inter-American Eco-
    nomic Affairs, XXIV, 1 (Summer, 1970).

Heller, Jack. "Development Assistance Strategies in
    Latin America." Development Digest, VIII, 3
    (July, 1970).

Herrera, Felipe, and others. Una Década de Lucha por
    América Latina. Mexico D.F.: Fondo de Cultura
    Económica, 1970.

IBRD. The World Bank, IDA and IFC: Policies and
    Operations. Washington, D.C., April, 1968.

_____. 100 Questions and Answers. Washington,
    D.C., March, 1970.

IDA. 50 Questions and Answers. Washington, D.C.,
    May, 1970.

IDB. Agreement Establishing the Inter-American De-
    velopment Bank. Washington, D.C., April, 1959.

_____. Analysis of the Possible Formation of a
    Regional Finance Corporation for the Expansion
    of Latin American Industry. Washington, D.C.,
    August, 1970.

_____. _Annual Report_. Washington, D.C., 1960-70.

_____. Group of Controllers of the Review and Evaluation System. _Study of Sources and Uses of Funds_. CRE 1/69-Rev. 2. Washington, D.C., August, 1969.

_____. _Multinational Investment in the Economic Development and Integration of Latin America_. Washington, D.C., April, 1968.

_____. _Proposal for an Increase in the Resources of the Inter-American Development Bank_. Washington, D.C., April, 1970.

Lowenthal, Abraham F. "Alliance Rhetoric Versus Latin American Reality." _Foreign Affairs_ (April, 1970).

Maschke, Arturo. _La Creación del Banco Interamericano de Desarrollo_. Mexico D.F.: Centro de Estudios Monetarios Latinoamericanos, 1966.

Mikesell, Raymond F. _Foreign Investments in Latin America_. Washington, D.C.: Pan American Union, 1955.

OAS. "Act of Bogotá." _Final Report of the Secretary-General of the Organization of American States on the Third Meeting of the Special Committee to Study the Formulation of New Measures for Economic Cooperation_. OEA/Ser. G/IV/C-i-487, Rev. 2. Washington, D.C., 1960.

_____. "Alliance for Progress." _Official Documents Emanating from the Special Meeting of the Inter-American Economic and Social Council at the Ministerial Level_. OEA/Ser. H/XII.L. Washington, D.C., 1961.

_____. _External Financing for Latin American Development_. OEA/Ser. H/X.14, CIES/1382. Washington, D.C., May, 1969.

Operación Panamericana: Compilación de Documentos--
    VI. Rio de Janeiro: Presidência da República,
    Serviço de Documentação, 1960.

Prebisch, Raúl. Change and Development. Washington,
    D.C.: IDB, 1970.

Singh, Manmohan. Regional Development Banks. New
    York: Carnegie Endowment for International
    Peace, 1970.

U.N. International Cooperation in a Latin American
    Development Policy (U.N. Sales No.: 1954.II.G.2),
    September, 1954.

White, John. Regional Development Banks. London:
    Overseas Development Institute, 1971.

SIDNEY DELL has been working on problems of trade and development for more than 25 years. A British citizen, he was trained in economics at Oxford University. After war service, he went to the British Board of Trade as an economist and subsequently joined the United Nations Secretariat. Since 1964, he has been Director of the New York Office of the United Nations Conference on Trade and Development (UNCTAD), dealing with problems of development financing.

His other books include Trade Blocs and Common Markets (New York: Alfred Knopf, 1963) and A Latin American Common Market? (New York: Oxford University Press, 1966).